Tideflats to Tomorrow:

The History of Seattle's SoDo

BY Dan Raley

Publisher & Editor: Jeff Shelley
Book Design, Layout & Contemporary Photos: Anni Shelley
Printed in the United States of America by Consolidated Press (SoDo)

Published by:
Fairgreens Publishing, LLC
270 South Hanford Street, Suite 100
Seattle, Washington 98134
(206) 522-6981
Email: fairgreens@seanet.com
To order, visit www.fairgreenspublishing.com.

ISBN: 978-0-615-33823-1

Library of Congress Control Number: 2009943579

*This book is dedicated to all the
hard-working people of SoDo.*

Table of Contents

Acknowledgements

SoDo was like a blind date that worked out better than expected. When my friend Jeff Shelley called and said he was looking for someone to write a book about Seattle's industrial area, my first reaction was this: What am I getting into?

SoDo wasn't all that attractive on the outside. SoDo was never going to win any beauty contests. SoDo didn't exactly make heads turn. Yet I'm a sucker for personality, and this rough-around-the-edges part of town had plenty of that. Soon I was smitten. After three months, I knew nearly everything there was to know about this rectangular-shaped neighborhood. I felt like we had been friends for a long time, SoDo and I.

I want to thank Henry Liebman, a sometimes controversial man who owns much of this real estate, for having the desire to put something about this place on record, unencumbered by any unrealistic demands.

Shelley, who spearheaded the project and thought of me when there were many other writer choices, deserves my gratitude as well. The man knows what he wants and gets things done.

The fourth wheel in this effort, Anni Shelley, dressed up everything with her clever designs, and I salute her for that.

SoDo and I have become inseparable, largely because of the interesting people I met while trolling its streets. James Dillon, Mike Peringer, Frank Stagen, John Cochrane, Dave Ederer, Bill Rabel, Bill Rosen, Doug Rosen, Robb Stack, Art Mendelsohn, Frank Firmani, Rick Osterhout, Dave Rost, Scott Soules, Hal Amick, Scott Andrews, Mick McCoy, Rex Holt, Bruce Eastes, Gary Eastes, John Bennett, Tom O'Keefe, Paul Vetters, Jeffrey Long, Bill Rabel, Doug Glant, Dave Gering and Andy Yurkanin were among the countless souls who treated me to a walking tour, car tour or sit-down conversation, sharing their insights and giving me inspiration.

Admittedly, SoDo and I likely will drift apart, as I move in the direction of other book projects, yet what a great blind date.

Dan Raley

Foreword

By Paul Dorpat

Oh, to Go to SoDo

Trusted to write the foreward to the book you hold, I might have gone anywhere that is roughly on subject, but I'm staying on the SoDo tideflats and will not stray. Dan Raley, the author, will describe how the name came to be and what a serendipitous gift it was to have that "Do" in SoDo nesting both downtown and in the Kingdome – the short-lived Kingdome.

For newcomers with no SoDo memory before the current millennium, we will describe the Kingdome as one of history's largest domes. Some with appetite for the monumental think that it resembled a super hamburger. But really its roof was less like a bun than a crustacean. That and its leaks were better fitting for a tideflat. Dedicated in the spring of 1976, the Kingdome was still a teenager when its ceiling began to fall to pieces in 1994. One day short of its 24th birthday the concrete colossus was strung with explosives like popcorn on a Christmas tree and spectacularly imploded. Again, Raley will describe all this, no doubt, in thrilling detail.

Before there was a Kingdome south of King Street the principal lures on the old tideflats – as I used them – were the Post Office transfer station on Lander where one delivered both eleventh-hour grant applications and almost-late tax payments; Sears (for me the chocolate-covered orange sticks at the candy counter) nearby at Utah and Lander; and Pacific Iron and Metal, also nearby on 4th Avenue South. That last was something like an industrial-sized garage sale. For most, the tideflat neighborhood was scarcely noticed as they sped to the airport along Interstate 5 and the Alaska Way freeway past the flat and yet

Paul Dorpat at the downtown waterfront with seagulls and Seattle icon Ivar.

oddly rolling acres of railroad tracks and warehouse avenues. The Kingdome changed that. Once raised 250 feet above its own 50-yard line, this original "north pole" of SoDo became Seattle's first really big-league landmark and tideland destination.

Staying on the tideflats, I'll now share a reminiscence in which the Dome plays a big part and I a small one.

Soon after the Kingdome was dedicated a distracted filmmaker set on my studio table a box filled with developed but unedited 16mm footage for a film he'd been commissioned to assemble on the Dome's construction. It took a lot of innovative assembling to put up the largest concrete dome this side of the moon. For unexplained reasons, the visitor asked me to complete the film and I agreed. I discovered soon enough that what he left with me resembled raw material for an episode of "Industry on Parade," a documentary TV series that was free to TV stations and semi-popular in the 1950s. So I set about adding to his construction footage some hand-held spectacles of the completed Kingdome at play. Surely, I thought, the game-time banging of footballers shot from near the Seahawks' bench would do the trick. Kingdome management, the client, agreed.

I was told to come before the next Seahawks game and ring a marked bell placed beside what I remember as a regular-sized door set or framed into a much larger door – one easily big enough for elephants and competition tractors – that led directly to the floor of the Kingdome. I rang, the door opened, someone without a word directed me to the running track and then disappeared. Above and to all sides of me were 66,000 uncannily silent fans.

I should have stayed on the track. Instead I stupidly started walking – wobbling really – directly for the players' bench across the acre of Astroturf that separated us. It was then that the fans arose from their rows and began to sing as one the national anthem. With the first line, "Oh say can you see," I was certain that what they saw was the only moving thing on the stadium floor: me.

I was, I thought, also the only person not singing and felt that from the stadium's concrete-ramparts fans were examining me for patriotism or lack of it. The synthetic grass was made for cleats not tennis shoes, and with every Astro-step I either teetered to the left or tottered to the right. My knees were wobbling and I might have collapsed except that I was saved by history – tidelands history. It happened like this.

When the anthem-singing fans came to the proud lyrics "gave proof through the night that our flag was still there" I heard, as it were, city founder Arthur Denny's Bell still peeling nearby on the tideflats from the deck of the sailing ship, the bark *Brontes*. The famous bell was en route in 1861 from New England to Seattle to ring for classes and much else from the cupola prepared for it atop the community's brand-new University of Washington. The *Brontes* had missed Yesler's wharf in a Puget Sound fog and came aground at low tide, most likely on the first prominent sand spit south of King Street. There it clanged for help. That spit straddled the future

Dearborn Street east of Occidental Avenue, exactly where they later built the Kingdome, and so also where I made my wobbly way to the team bench. Thankfully, with my amused hallucination of the bells plaintive ringing, strength returned to my knees and I made it to the footballers without the assistance of any sports medicine.

Many years after the *Brontes* rescue, that sand spit was home for hundreds of squatters and jumpers during Seattle's big boom-bust-boom years, beginning in the mid-1880s. The down-and-out among them – the majority – stayed until forced out in the early 20th Century by the railroads and their publicly funded sheriffs. In 1902, while reflecting on how this "riff-raff" might be moved, the Seattle Times revealed, "There are probably not less than 2,000 shacks scattered over the flats southof the city." (This rent-free improvised community was, of course, assembled from scrap again during the "Great Depression" of the 1930s and the future SoDo was again spotted with shacks and Rube Goldberg communities called Hoovervilles in honor of the president "in charge" when the wealth of nations crashed in 1929.)

A much smaller group who frequented the tideflats beginning in the 1880s were the warring speculators who hoped to establish precedents by making marks in the sand. One jumper drove piles into the tideflats during the day while another pulled them up at night. Some protested that they were only preparing oyster beds, and the tidelands "oyster wars" that followed were sometimes violent. More to the point, the oysters themselves were irritated. It was widely understood that when Seattle pioneer Doc Maynard first tried to nurture oysters on the Elliott Bay tideflats he found that Duwamish River silt prevented it. The latter-day tideflat oyster farmers were phony real estate speculators who consistently sited their beds as close to King Street and the city as they could mark them.

Reclaiming the tidelands first began in the early 1850s to all sides of Henry Yesler's lumber mill with its own sawdust. Next, a waste stream of contributors – including scavenger wagons, stuff from construction sites, dead horses and later railroad droppings – extended the fill south into the tideflats. Raising the tidelands got systematic in the mid-1890s when former state governor Eugene Semple convinced the legislature to let him start dredging the shallow and close-in parts of Elliott Bay and, by pipeline, distribute the vacuumed mud to mattresses of boards and brush behind which some of it would hold long enough to drain and build saleable land.

In addition to his reclamation fees, Semple would earn some of that "made" land from the state, which took ownership of the tidelands from the federal government with statehood in 1889.

In 1895 the Argus, a long-lived weekly hereabouts, advised, "Probably no one with a business eye has viewed the tidelands which stretch across the head of Elliott Bay without being struck by the vast possibilities that lie undeveloped therein. Upon this new land would spring up myriad of lumber and shingle mills, warehouses, elevators and industrial developments of many kinds whose smokestacks would rival the firs of the neighboring hills."

By 1895 the firs were hard to remember, but a few smoke-stacks already rose from the shoreline below Beacon Hill and above the timber quays built over the tidelands, but none yet directly above filled land. As it developed, the most important tideland developers were not factories but railroads. In the mid-1890s, secret agents for the Great Northern – the railroad with a goat for a mascot – began to quietly gobble at what tidelands bargains they could in preparation for the building of the rail-road's yards south of King Street and, in 1906, the dedication of its grand Venetian-styled depot on it. The GN was so quiet about its purchases that, on a few occasions, its secret agents wound up in bidding contests for the same piece of tidelands. Real estate agent H.H. Dearborn (of the namesake street) advertised, "Get the Tidelands Habit," and Dearborn had tidelands to sell.

A sampler of headlines and PR slogans embraced by the dailies suggests the excitement then: "Fortune wrested from the tides"; "Making the tidelands habitable"; "How Seattle pushed back the sea"; "Future factory land"; "A new city on the tidelands"; "Seattle's new smokestack neighborhood."

Reaching across a centerfold, Dearborn's ad banner advised buyers, "Get the Tidelands Habit" and concluded "It will Make You Money While You Sleep." He might have added, "But probably not tonight."

It took years for the GN to buy up about one-third of the tideflats, build that sumptuous depot and reach it through a tunnel beneath the central business district. During those years, tideland hysteria continued to behave like the flu, passing between sweats and chills. During one hot stretch tideland futures looked so promising that the Duwamish River was split at its mouth into east and west waterways and a new tideland raised between them. It was called Harbor Island, which was a good name only by half. Through its first years the principle pecking order on the worlds' largest man-made island was not between competitors but among chicken farmer Charles Butler's birds – about 300 of them – whose eggs twice a week he rowed to market.

Union Depot opened in 1906 but not with pomp and circum-stance. Debris was still on the floor of the waiting room and the walks and roads to the depot were not yet paved. By then about 7 million cubic yards of mud had been dredged for the making of the two waterways. The island between them was raised to a safe 18 inches above maximum high tide, but there was still no bridge to Butler's birds.

When "final grades" were set for the tidelands it was expected that the long-awaited forest of smokestacks was at hand. To avoid disrupting the several railroads' easy access to the coming factories, higher grades were set for the vehicular avenues running north and south through the future SoDo. If this planning had not been wisely abandoned, SoDo might now be a neighborhood of trestles. Instead, it was discovered that most of the smokestacks on the tideflats were the moving kind atop steam engines. Warehouses would dominate this "industrial park," not factories, and the separated grades were forsaken with considerable savings. Streets and rails could share the same grade, except at a few bottlenecks, but those were south of Spokane Street and so also south of SoDo.

By now, SoDo generally either smells sweet or does not smell at all. It wasn't so for the pioneers, who knew the difference between the fresh salted air coming off the tide-splashed central waterfront and the stinks curling north from the great brackish puddle south of King Street. Once reclaimed and dried out and then foot-printed with warehouses and lighter industry, the general rank aroma abandoned the tideflats.

In 1980, I became a modern squatter in SoDo as I moved my studio with 10 other artists to the top floor of the Cork Insulation building on 1st Avenue South, a very long block north of Sears. It was low-cost rent and those orange sticks at Sears were cheap, too.

One hot summer afternoon, with the four-year-old Kingdome on my right, I pushed an eccentric metal filing cabinet on its own wheels through the empty Sunday streets of SoDo. I bought it, of course, at the Salvation Army thrift shop on 4th Avenue South.

Heading for my new studio and rolling through the sizzling reclaimed tideland on an exceptionally hot August weekend, I might have confused the undulating in the SoDo avenues for optical effects of the radiating heat. But I knew better and, as with the sounding of Denny's Bell, it was tideland history that straightened me. The undulating was from fill slowly sinking at different rates, and it continues to.

Postscript: The Denny Bell that rang from SoDo in 1862 survives in the cupola atop Denny Hall on the University of Washington campus and can still ring when it is not chained.

Introduction:

SoDo, What's that?

Dressing for a game at Safeco field, the popular baseball player pleaded total ignorance when asked what it meant. He grimaced and shrugged. He had no clue this was the actual name of his athletic workplace for the past two decades, that the neighborhood surrounding him on all sides was christened in this manner the same year he was called to the big leagues by the Mariners as a teenage kid with a big smile and even bigger bat.

SoDo?

Ken Griffey Jr. knows all about it now, as does everyone else who works and plays in Seattle.

It's an ever-changing place with character and characters, much more than aging warehouses and machine shops sitting pensively in the shadows of expensive sports stadiums. It's no longer the awkward cousin that nobody invites to family gatherings anymore for fear he'll track up the carpets with his dirty shoes. Mostly, it's a long ignored part of town that wants to be seen and heard, and people finally are paying attention.

There is coffee of all kinds to be had there, in close proximity to stores full of fresh donuts. There are new buildings replacing ones that are a century old. There is nightlife that is as cool and chic as anywhere in a town that famously spawned the unforgettable sounds of Ray Charles, Jimi Hendrix and Kurt Cobain.

SoDo has become such a valuable piece of property that people are fighting over it rather than rudely ignoring it. The sitting American President swears by it, even campaigned inside it. Light-rail trains zip through the middle of it when there once might have been good reason to go around it.

The story of SoDo is about an unsophisticated part of Seattle coming of age, of a place standing up and demanding to be counted among the more exclusive corners of the port city that governs it. There are far too many junkyards spilling all over the place and roads of shifting or no asphalt that might never get fixed, but this place has a certain charm and charisma to it.

If there is any radical new look to Seattle over the next 10 to 20 years it will come from SoDo, which could be the big bushy mustache or a nose ring suddenly protruding from the city's otherwise familiar features.

SoDo?

Ken Griffey Jr. can tell you about this place now. It's grown up, just like he is.

SoDo, or South of Downtown, is a collection of four square miles of trucks, trains, ships and shops. It wears Seattle's hardhats and coveralls, and it's a grimy and sweaty place.

It's the city's fiercely protected industrial center that wants to be much more as it experiences continual growing pains. It's a massive grid of low-slung buildings that wouldn't mind mixing with a few mid- or high-rises.

It's a rectangular-shaped community that offers the following tourist attractions: the biggest building in town, the worst streets, the first Costco store site (occupied by yet another remodeled warehouse), the worst traffic, the old Rainier brewery and a billion dollars worth of professional sports stadiums.

Early-day photo of Seattle's waterfront; view from Beacon Hill, circa 1881.

One hundred and fifteen years ago, SoDo was just a big puddle. This salty part of town was nothing more than saltwater.

Seattle's Atlantis

In its rawest form, this neighborhood was protruding mounds and ridges of silt and sediment that were visible at low tide but would completely disappear under six to 16 feet of water lapping up to what is now Interstate 5. It was Seattle's Atlantis. Not a lost city rising from the depths, but a new addition created by dumping recycled dirt into those depths. Not a link to a forgotten past, but the connection to a mapped-out future that would rest only on solid ground – or at least as firm as they could make it.

Initially, rickety piers in no particular order would crisscross this liquid lowland that stretched over 2,000 acres at the south end of town. Equally flimsy buildings would be constructed on these makeshift stilts, housing start-up businesses and factories that meandered through the tideflats and couldn't possibly have had chronological addresses. With everything thrown together, little care was given to aesthetics or productiveness. The loud expletives repeatedly emanating from this crude and teetering community would be workers agonizing when their tools slipped between the open creases in the wooden floors and suddenly disappeared with a splash into the water below.

As the tide covered and uncovered this uneven ground twice daily, giving a chameleon-like appearance to Seattle's southern waterfront, people envisioned something better. People demanded something better, so they started building something far better.

On to the Future

Shipping was a natural industry for this port, but shipping proved a challenge.

The loud expletives repeatedly emanating from this crude and teetering community would be workers agonizing when their tools slipped between the open creases in the wooden floors and suddenly disappeared with a splash into the water below.

Different-sized piers and the shallow harbor bottom created an unnecessary challenge for incoming vessels to negotiate. A Japanese steamship line was contracted to deliver tea, paper, silk, matting and curios to the city, and leave with lumber, fish, tobacco, raw cotton and manufactured goods. Those in charge of the city realized something had to be done to further encourage this lucrative foreign commerce, not sink it or leave it stuck in the mud.

One of the meatiest provisions for Washington receiving statehood in 1889 was an effective settlement of these tidelands: foremost dealing with what is now called SoDo. Washington, the northwestern-most territory converted into the 42nd state of the union, demonstrated ample potential by connecting Elliott Bay to Puget Sound and the Pacific Ocean, but it needed to maximize the economic possibilities to truly be successful and livable.

One sure way to do this was to rearrange the waterfront of its biggest city in orderly fashion. Seattle, in its fourth decade of existence and suffering the similar plight of a middle-aged man, was physically out of shape in multiple ways. It was too fat in some places, too lean in others. The downtown area was squeezed by steep hills on one side and those marshy tidelands on the other.

Henry Yesler

Decision Time

Two things happened to build some civic muscle: 1) New state leaders declared that all waterfront properties, including piers, dock sites and designated harbor lines belonged to the government, not the private citizens who occupied them, and would fall under the jurisdiction of a newly created, five-member harbor commission; and 2) city policy-makers determined

they would knock down parts of the more elevated sections of the city – among them Denny Hill, Jackson Hill and Beacon Hill – and deposit the fill into the lowest area, a place now recognized as SoDo. This would make the downtown landscape far more expansive and uniform.

Once these ambitious plans were unveiled, one particular Seattle industry experienced an immediate groundswell in business: law offices became in great demand. Attorneys were hired. Lawsuits filled the courts. In 1890 and 1891, injunctions were filed by Henry Yesler, Columbia and Puget Sound Railway Company,

> *Horse-drawn wagons were lined up like so many modern-day dump trucks, accepting walls of dirt scraped off hillsides and fastidiously delivering them to the tideflats.*

Seattle Terminal Railway and Elevator Company, Stimson Mill Company, Seattle, Lake Shore and Eastern Railway and Schwabacher Brothers and Company, each holding land claims and operating businesses. All were declared trespassers by the state, but they wouldn't give in easily.

Yesler, who has several Seattle landmarks named after him, was one of the city's earliest settlers. He arrived from Portland 40 years earlier and built a waterfront sawmill about two blocks north from what is SoDo. He filed the first harbor reclamation suit and fought this thing as far as it would go. A litigious man as it turned out, Yesler received an injunction from King County Superior Court only to have it overturned on appeal by the state Supreme Court and that negative ruling upheld by the U.S. Supreme Court, effectively ending all other legal opposition to the state land grab.

Shoving the Dirt Around

The great SoDo earth-move began in earnest in 1895. Horse-drawn wagons were lined up like so many modern-day dump trucks, accepting walls of dirt scraped off hillsides and fastidiously delivering them to the tideflats. As people became more creative with this monotonous and weighty task, they laid down long sections of large pipes and chutes in which to water-blast, or sluice, a mixture of

Eugene Semple

water and soil called slurry directly overland and into the bay.

SoDo, like Rome, wasn't built in a day. It took 20 years to fill more than half of the tidelands and $20 million to pay for it. There were constant interruptions, with people needing to wade through periodic legal challenges as well as the murky waters. Similar to a country club member, new waterfront landowners had to pay assessments on any improvements, and liens against their property were used to enforce these edicts. The people doing the digging and filling around their properties were the recipients. At one point, the landowners stopped paying and big lawsuits resulted, forcing the hands of the losers to resume paying.

Jackson Street Regrade looking north.

Taking the Lead

One who took advantage of this potential money-making opportunity was Eugene Semple. He had been Washington's territorial governor and an unsuccessful candidate to become the first state governor. He was one of the five original appointees to the harbor commission, and was now on the other side. He resigned from the commission and enlisted others to create the Seattle and Lake Washington Waterways Company. It was Semple's intention to build a canal through Beacon Hill connecting Lake Washington and the waterfront, filling in the tideflats as he went.

After lining up financial backers in St. Louis, he dug into the hillside until two things got in the way: He ran out of money and encountered rock deposits. Modern-day evidence remains, with a divot in Beacon Hill clearly visible above Spokane Street. Still, Semple, who died in 1908, deserves much of the credit for filling in the first 1,400 acres of what is now SoDo. At low tide, his company dug two and a half miles of waterways that were 40 to 50 feet deep and 500 to 1,000 feet wide, and installed much of the seven miles of bulkheads that kept everything in place.

As the ground level of SoDo began to take shape, city engineer Reginald Thomson became heavily involved. He decreed that all piers and wharves would be built in a line that moved from southeast to northwest, creating a much needed configuration for shipping. The old piers had to come down anyway. Constructed out of cheap materials, they were ravaged by marine insects and prone to fire or falling down.

Free Fill Here

Finding tideland fill was no problem. The intersection of Fourth Avenue and Blanchard Street was lowered 107 feet. The intersection of Fifth and Blanchard dropped 93 feet. From the Denny Regrade project alone, 5 million cubic yards of soil were excavated and poured into the tidelands. Another 5 million cubic yards, pulled from 50 city blocks, were delivered from the Jackson Regrade effort.

In the midst of all this massive dirt transfer, controversy erupted. There were people such as Semple, who favored building a ship canal in South Seattle through Beacon Hill – rather than in the north end of the city – because it meant easier access to waste materials earmarked for filling in the tidelands. It made no difference that the southern route was nearly five miles longer to traverse than the one proposed through Ballard and Shilshole Bay. Public opinion was enthusiastically in favor of the plan, if for no other reason than to simply get things done.

A New Concept

Three Seattle judges, Roger Greene, John McGilvra and Thomas Burke, lobbied hard for the more economical

"I had half of that property, all tidelands. I said anybody who wants to drop off their rubble, let them do it. It's good, solid rubble in there. You couldn't run a bulldozer through there now. That's one of the ways I got it filled for cheap."

Harold Stack

northern route instead, and good sense prevailed, with Seattle newspapers and the Chamber of Commerce changing their positions as well as other minds. Greene gave 11 reasons why a South Seattle ship canal should be rejected, with none more accusatory and persuasive than the 11th and following claim:

"The main purpose of the south canal promoters would seem to be not marine communication with Lake Washington but cheap and abundant material for filling

mudflats. They fall down when they try to serve two masters. Their main purpose determines the site of the excavation. Facility and convenience of intercommunication with the sea are lost or are not impartially considered. But a cut of drastic depth and proportions must be certainty, what, if any, are the quicksands, the sliding clays, the shapes and slopes, that may be met with among the assorted masses of glacial moraine, which constitutes the interaqueous barrier and without primary and sufficiently intelligent consideration and comprehension of the present and future commercial necessities of the city."

Ah, the Future

Once filled in, SoDo would become a steady string of shipyards and steel mills, launched along the waterfront largely for war-time needs. "Machinery Row" filled up First Avenue South. "Produce Row" swept up Occidental Avenue South. Manufacturing sprouted everywhere else. Cement and brick buildings replaced the wooden ones that were a constant fire hazard. Sears and Roebuck, Ederer Crane, Star Machinery, Peat Belting, Alaskan Copper Works, Stack Steel, and Pacific Iron and Metal would become neighborhood staples, with some still open for business today.

Parts of 6th Avenue South were thick marshlands in several spots until the 1949 Seattle earthquake helped accelerate the solidifying process as a gesture of goodwill that had economical foresight attached to it.

"The area had a lot of brick buildings fall down," said Harold Stack, who operated the now-closed Stack Steel and still owns several acres of SoDo landscape. "I had half of that property, all tidelands. I said anybody who wants to drop off their rubble, let them do it. It's good, solid rubble in there. You couldn't run a bulldozer through there

now. That's one of the ways I got it filled for cheap."

Gradually, SoDo's water-front offerings would disappear or change shape as world wars, the Great Depression and general modernization would alter business operations before the Port of Seattle acquired it all, paved it over and created a super-terminal that would have made the original statehood leaders proud.

All That's New . . .

In modern times SoDo sits on 100 feet of soil in some places. Ninety-five feet of it is fill; the other five is bedrock. The ground is so unstable one new building under construction in 2009 to be used for retail and light-industrial required 276 pilings driven to bedrock to satisfy modern earthquake regulations.

. . . Is Still the Same

Not everyone, of course, does business on such a reinforced foundation.

The Pacific Coast Feather Company, one of the nation's leading producers of feather bedding and formerly a mattress and outerwear manufacturer, is headquartered in a sprawling three-story building that sits at 1964 4th Avenue South, on a street that runs down the middle of the SoDo district.

Founded in the 1920s and owned by the Hanauer family since 1940, Pacific Coast Feather is the largest handler of down material in the world. The company imports goose feathers in compressed bales from China and has them cleaned at a factory in Marysville, Wash., a process that requires eight washings. From there, the feathers are shipped to any one of 12 plants nationally, including one in Kent, south of Seattle.

The original Pacific Coast Feather building, located a few long blocks from Safeco Field, the modern home of the Seattle Mariners, consists mostly of office space.

However, a tour conducted by Jeffrey Long, the long-time executive assistant to the deceased Jerry Hanauer and a building caretaker of sorts, reveals some bedding products stockpiled at the main office site.

A self-described history buff, Long is keenly aware of Sodo's underwater origins. He shows off the basement level of the building to a visitor. He points to the rolling concrete floor and explains why it has buckled. He says what's beneath it might surprise you. Crossing the room and pulling out a set of keys Long unlocks an otherwise unnoticeable basement door, which is maybe 15 feet below street level. A sheet of cardboard prevents anyone from slipping into darkness and tumbling to the absolute bottom.

Long pulls out a flashlight and shines it on the black vacuum below. It smells of saltwater. Depending on the time of day, it is often covered with just that. This is nowhere near the waterfront and practically next door to where American League baseball games are held all summer long.

This is part of the 2,000 acres of yearling Seattle that apparently escaped capture well over a century ago.

Considering where it's located, this is still an underground and watery world that crosses under the busy, concrete- and asphalt-covered one overhead, namely three busy streets and two sets of railroad tracks.

This is where so many turn-of-the-century men worked hard sluicing, hauling, dumping and arguing.

Guess what? They missed a spot.

"There's some tideflat for you," Long said, pointing to the shimmering surface below.

Peering into Puget Sound tideflats underneath Pacific Coast Feather Company in 2009.

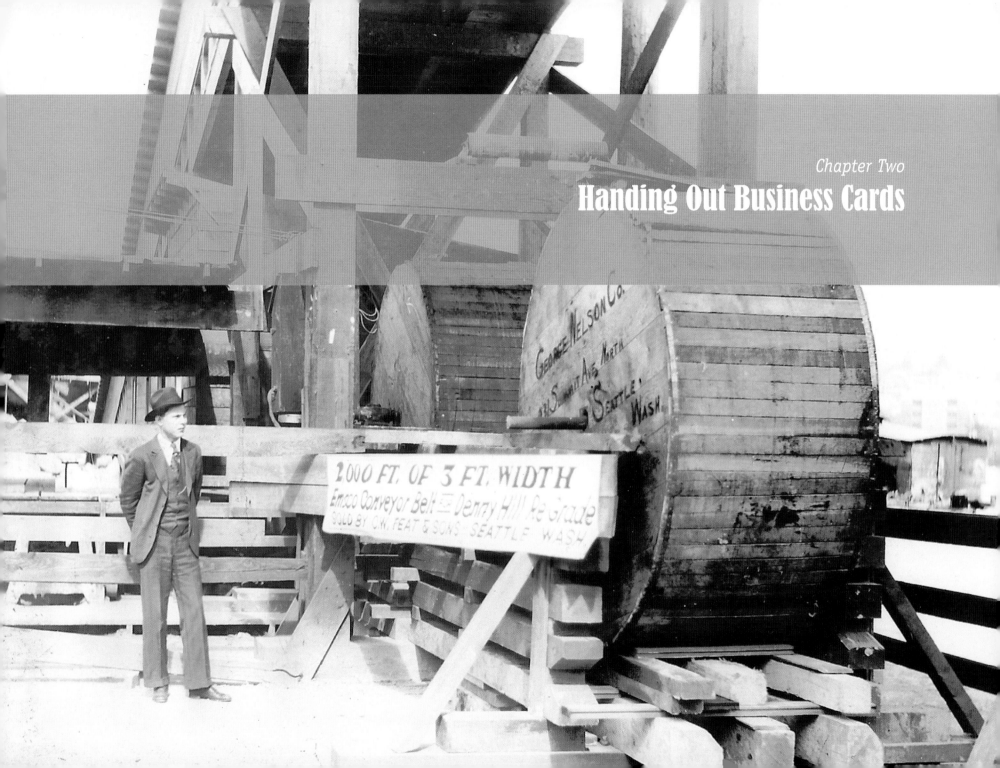

The modest building at 115 Weller Street couldn't have been more than 10 feet wide or twice that tall. It had a solitary window next to the front door, three planks that provided a make-shift sidewalk, a yard full of equipment and a sign in white letters, punctuated with a star on each side, which read: Office of Star Machinery Co.

The photo is dated 1900. Standing in the doorway and posing for what appeared to be a rare promotional pho-tograph for the times, hands stuck in his coat pockets, was Johan "Christian" Rabel. He wears a derby hat, bow tie and his Sunday best, with a watch chain peaking out of his turn-of-the-century fashion

ensemble. Rabel was a German immigrant drawn to America for opportunity, pulled out West like so many others by the lure of the Alaska Gold Rush, and ultimately content with going no farther than Seattle to make a comfortable living and realize his dreams.

Rabel not only sold used sawmill equipment out of these cramped quarters, he created a business venture like no other in what is now the city's SoDo District: the longest-running company in the neighborhood, 109 years and counting.

A Star is Born

His business model, always family-owned and carrying only SoDo-centric addresses, would alter its service ap-proach, morphing from strictly sales to a combined manufacturing plant and rentals to, today, only rent-als. It would expand a couple of times, opening a state-of-the-art plant in 1953 and then downsizing with the shift in industry dynamics to overseas' offerings. It would change its name to Star Rentals. It would provide five generations of Rabels – and

Christian Rabel, the founder of Star Machinery, which later became Star Rentals.

still counting – with a pay-check, defying traditional odds.

Relatives usually don't get along so well for so long, especially when making money is involved.

"We've met with consul-tants and read business books and there's a curse with a family business, and that curse seldom goes past three generations," commented Bill Rabel, the great-grandson of Christian Rabel and current co-owner of Star Rentals with his brothers Leigh and John, who succeeded their father, Irvine Rabel, who followed his father Otto and uncle Vic. "Our operating mode is 'Don't screw it up.'"

"The company has changed over the years, but it's still here," said Christian Rabel, one of Bill Rabel's two sons and the modern-day namesake of the company's founder. "It's nice to have all those connec-tions."

So why call it Star Machin-ery and Star Rentals? Why not Rabel Machinery, or Rabel and Sons? The original Christian Rabel admittedly didn't come up with an original idea when it was time to choose the company moniker. He didn't consult the celestial spheres above to make "Star" the longstanding brand name with service connotations.

He simply took one look around his Weller Street headquarters and claimed what was handy.

"He realized he needed to come up with a name, and it needed to be short, easy to remember and with a good visual image," Bill Rabel explained. "He glanced down toward the corner of the little shack that was his office and he saw an empty crate from Star Cut-Plug Tobacco. That's how Star Machinery was named."

The company star in the logo, later accompanied by the words "Symbol of Service," was colored red until the mid-1950s, when it was deemed politically incorrect because of the ongoing McCarthy Hearings

and the country's vigorous anti-Communist crusade. The star has been white ever since.

"We redesigned the logo so there wasn't a taint of having a red star," Bill Rabel said. "That was Russian. That was Communist."

> *"He realized he needed to come up with a name, and it needed to be short, easy to remember and with a good visual image. He glanced down toward the corner of the little shack that was his office and he saw an empty crate from Star Cut-Plug Tobacco. That's how Star Machinery was named."*
>
> Bill Rabel

Modern-day view of Star Rentals.

Over a Century & Counting

Christian Rabel moved his machinery business to 1741 1st Avenue South in 1906, and opened a rental shop at 201 South Horton Street in 1916. The initial Weller Street location today is buried beneath Qwest Field, home to the NFL's Seattle Seahawks.

Experiencing a fairly sizeable post-World War

II surge in business, Rabel's descendents built a huge 50,000-square-foot plant at 241 South Lander Street, one that had unlimited space for machinery exhibits to appease customers and a place promoted as one-of-a-kind in the U.S.

"The new building not only is the result of a business increase of 33 percent in the territory we serve –

Washington, Oregon, Northern Idaho, Western Montana and Alaska – but demonstrates our faith in the continued growth in Seattle," Rabel's son, Irvine, proclaimed at the time of the store's 1953 unveiling.

That faith lasted three and a half decades. The Rabels remained in the machinery business until the late 1980s, finally shutting down those operations for two reasons: 1) cheaper foreign production had undercut the American market; and 2) their rental business was growing rapidly.

Today, Star Rentals is located at 1919 4th Avenue South, the hub of a 17-store chain that runs throughout Washington and Oregon. The current outlet is a "U-shaped" facility with a huge sign sporting a proper white star against a red backdrop, planted amid rows of heavy equipment lined up uniformly within a fenced-in enclosure. The rental yard sits just around the corner from the company's old ma-

chinery plant on South Lander Street, since remodeled and now home to the Northwest Pacific Galleries Antique Mall.

The Rabels keep their corporate offices in Leschi, overlooking Lake Washington. Inside is hung a stately painting of Christian Rabel, bespectacled, well-groomed and stern in expression. His great-grandsons can't offer many particulars or insights about the man, other than he was a journeyman machinist who was fairly resolute in making sure the family business was a big success, far from his homeland, and he did just that.

"I guess he was wound pretty tight, a typical German," Bill Rabel surmises.

SoDo Lineage

Star Rentals is one of nine family-owned companies that have popped up in Seattle's most concentrated industrial district and conducted business for nine decades or more. Many of them, but not

They provided their families with a long-running Northwest legacy that has accompanied Seattle as it moved from a horse-and-buggy town to a place that builds jets, makes coffee and creates computer software.

all, remain in operation in some manner, some still in the hands of the same lineage. Others making the list of SoDo's most distinguished and resilient are: Ederer Crane (108 years – as of 2009), O.B. Williams Company (107), Peat Belting (102), Markey Machinery (102), M. Bloch Company (101), Alaskan Copper Works (96), Amick Metal Fabricators (93) and Pacific Iron and Metal (91).

There's also Washington Iron Works, which was run for 89 years by the Frink Family

before it was sold, though 15 years of its business were conducted elsewhere in the city well before SoDo was filled in and created.

Add to that group the equally longstanding Sears and Roebuck (99 years) and Todd Shipyard (93), both corporately owned from the beginning, and SoDo has more generational lines to peruse than an old-growth evergreen tree.

Most of these long-running companies were opened by European immigrants drawn to Seattle by the 1897 Alaska Gold Rush, persuaded by the city's persistent and unapologetic self-promotion that everything was somehow connected from Puget Sound to the Yukon. Come to this progressive city, nationwide fliers promised, and get rich quick.

Most of these people created a personal fortune in a much slower and conservative fashion, putting down roots a couple thousand miles removed from the gold fields.

They provided their families with a long-running Northwest legacy that has accompanied Seattle as it moved from a horse-and-buggy town to a place that builds jets, makes coffee and creates computer software.

Seattle's Industrial Immigrants

German-born Edward Ederer was responsible for establishing Seattle's first milling shop, in 1901, setting up the Weber and Ederer Manufacturing Company on 2nd Avenue South. It eventually was turned into Ederer Crane and has been remade by modern-day family members into the uptown Ederer Investment Company. Edward Ederer's original intention was to run an Alaskan twine business, an offshoot of what his family members had developed in Chicago, which he did temporarily between milling jobs by creating Seattle Net and Twine Manufacturing.

"His intent was to go to Alaska and make fishing nets," said Dave Ederer of his great-grandfather. "He stayed in Seattle instead and bought the city's first engine lathe, and people found out and he had more work than he knew what to do with."

Ederer Crane would expand and become an international business, making cranes for all sorts of unusual jobs.

Edward Ederer, the founder of Ederer Crane. The portrait was done by John Taliaferro, one of the early members of the Puget Sound Group of Northwest Painters, founded in 1928. The portrait isn't dated, but was painted from a photo in the 1930's or '40s; Ederer died around 1925 at 71 or 72.

Production included the complete assembly of a crane and testing to certify that it worked as indicated. It was then disassembled and delivered to the customer.

The family retained control of this company until selling it in 1972, not long after Arthur Ederer, son of the founder and someone who took a turn at running the company, was killed in an unusual tragedy. Five years before Ederer Crane changed hands, 83-year-old Arthur left a winter luncheon at the Rainier Club in downtown Seattle. In his confusion, he made a wrong turn in his Lincoln Continental luxury automobile while heading home and drove down some railroad tracks. He got stuck in frigid temperatures and is believed to have died of hypothermia.

Still brandishing the original name under Minnesota-based ownership, Ederer Crane now conducts all of its manufacturing in Georgia because it's significantly cheaper to do so there,

but keeps its main office in Seattle, though no longer in SoDo. In 1999, post-family Ederer Crane was responsible for building the machinery that operates the retractable roof on the Seattle Mariners' Safeco Field, a job likened to creating "a reverse crane." At the same time, bright orange, green or yellow cranes bearing the family name are found in use worldwide, helping launch space shuttles and move nuclear waste.

Fourth- and fifth-generation Ederers, while invested in several businesses outside of SoDo, the city and around the country, maintain a neighborhood influence. They're owners of a half-dozen buildings in the industrial area that are leased to other businesses. They haven't abandoned the place altogether, though their corporate offices are located on the 30th floor of a downtown Seattle high-rise.

However, a fatigued Ederer Crane building, windows broken and siding coming apart, sits dark and inactive at 2937 South Utah Street, recently sold to yet another owner. This once-bustling industrial shop is full of classic old machinery and is used as a storage area for building materials pegged for nearby remodeling jobs. Ederer, in big block letters, is still highly visible across the top.

"It was fun to have it," said Dave Ederer, who worked at his great-grandfather's business from 1958 to 1965. "It was a company we've thought a number of times – and the brothers have five sons – that it would be nice to own again."

O.B. Here a Long Time

Owen Bulis "O.B." Williams was a Michigan man, the son of a Welsh immigrant, a boom-and-bust guy who arrived in Seattle in 1902 virtually penniless. He found stability selling residential doors in SoDo. In 1911, he moved into the same building at 1943 1st Avenue South that still carries

A 1905 advertisement showing the high-quality doors manufactured by O.B. Williams.

his name on the outside almost a century later, though the current door and sash company now occupies space once set aside for four businesses.

Williams died in the 1930s, leaving the company to his employees in his will. His wife, Hannah, however, contested that move in court and gained control of the business when a judge ruled that Williams hadn't sufficiently identified who constituted a deserving employee.

"She took over active management and kept all the employees, but they weren't all that happy after getting screwed out of ownership, so she decided to sell it," said Robert "Mickey" McCoy, an employee since 1948 and co-owner now with David Wick.

A door that once cost $3.50 now goes for $3,000. O.B. Williams is a full-service millworking outfit that also makes windows, cabinets, mouldings and wall paneling. It supplied all 3,000 panels for the inside of Benaroya

Hall. New York and Los Angeles architects love this place for its 5,000 cutting knives and other rare machinery. It's a far more complex operation than it once was.

"When we were in one building and whenever the phone rang we had to shut the machinery down, just to listen to the phone call," McCoy said.

When the Rubber Hits the Road

It took the 2001 earthquake to run Peat Belting out of SoDo, with its First Avenue South building slipping down seven feet during the shaker, leaving owner Rex Holt with the task of rebuilding or selling the site. He chose the latter, merging his company with Industrial Belt and Rubber, which was forced to give up its SoDo location near Harbor Island for imminent domain reasons related to the West Seattle freeway expansion. The combined businesses moved to Auburn under the second name.

The sign on this impressive machine reads: "2,000 feet of 3-feet width Emsco Conveyor Belt for Denny Hill Regrade. Sold by C.W. Peat & Sons, Seattle, Wash."

A lot of history left SoDo when Peat had to relocate. It was possibly Seattle's oldest running business, regardless of site, originally created as a leather-goods supplier in New York in the 1780s, moved to Port Angeles and Port Townsend shortly thereafter, and then turned up in Seattle under the direction of Charles Peat in 1899.

Peat Belting largely operated out of a former horse-and-buggy barn at 2430 1st Avenue South, a place built on pilings over tideflat fill, seven feet to be exact, or the amount of the foundation wiped out in the quake. Through the years all sorts of buggy parts, including buckboards and brass nameplates, were uncovered on the property and donated to Seattle's Museum of History and Industry. Early on, Peat

Belting was responsible for making all of the belts and conveyors that were used in the 20-year regrading of Seattle, with its product helping transfer the excavated dirt to barges and then to a dumping ground in what is now SoDo.

An earthquake sadly wasn't the only thing that rattled this business, with the site now a barren parking lot situated between Tiles for Less and SoDo Pop. Well after the turn of the century, Peat Belting was run by four family members, Charles "Eddie" Peat, and his sons, Ed, Harold and Alan. Incredibly, the eldest of these Peats was killed in a horrific accident. He was struck by a bus after having a few after-work drinks and leaving a popular watering hole, the since-closed Spiro's Café and Tavern, which was four doors away at 2700 1st Avenue South.

"He was drunk coming out of that corner bar," Holt confirmed of his grandfather, shaking his head at the memory.

The Machine Man

Charles Markey was another man pulled West by the bustling times ignited by the Alaska Gold Rush. In 1902, the Wisconsin native signed on as a junior engineer on the freighter *Centennial* that made regular Seattle-Alaska runs. Seeking more adventure, Markey built a schooner with partners and traveled up and down the Alaskan and Siberian coasts, trading as he went.

Charles Markey in a suit and tie working in his shop in 1929.

By 1907, Markey had turned to something a little less perilous and far more mainland. He started the C.H. Markey Machinery Company at the corner of Weller Street and Occidental Way, in the same general vicinity and time frame in which Christian Rabel of Star Machinery had begun his SoDo-area business pursuits.

Markey Machinery would flourish as a family-owned operation for the next nine decades, continuously expanding at its 79 South Horton Street plant and putting other Markeys – son Bill, grandsons Mike and Donn, and great grandson Gordon – on the payroll. Marine winches for tugboats and ships became the company's specialty, making it an industry leader.

In 1999, the business was sold by the Markeys to two long-term employees and Seattle natives, Blaine Dempke and Robert LeCoque, originally a draftsman and machinist, respectively, in effect keeping it in the family. Even after the change in ownership, Gordon Markey remains an employee, working as a union warehouseman.

In 2003, the company's beloved South Horton Street site was sold in favor of moving production to a cheaper facility in nearby Georgetown,

"I'm 95 and I'm still working, on the telephone only. My father started me and my brother, George, in the business and George's son, Dennis, is still in there, and my daughter's husband, Joel Richards, runs the new steel division, with a general oversight of the whole operation. It gives me an interest in living, and it's important to live. I don't know how much longer I'll have a reason. I just keep working."

Leo Bloch

leaving only the corporate offices behind in SoDo. Soon that connection will be gone, too. In 2010, Markey will have its office space and plant operations combined in Georgetown after undergoing site expansion, bringing all operations together in one place for the first time in 67 years.

"It's reluctantly," Dempke said of exiting SoDo, "but doing business on Horton wasn't without challenges with the trains."

A portrait of Moris (Morris) Bloch hangs in the office of Bloch Steel Industries in SoDo.

The Junk Man & His Sons

Latvian immigrant Morris Bloch, established the American Junk Company in 1905 on the Seattle waterfront and watched it slip into bankruptcy 16 years later, caused by him falling victim to influenza and a business partner's inattentiveness during his absence. He bounced back immediately by forming the M. Bloch Company and creating a metal recycler and steel wholesaler, still in operation at 4580 Colorado Avenue South, allowing him to pay off all his creditors. He also provided lasting careers for his two sons, which in Leo Bloch's case, has been forever.

"I'm 95 and I'm still working, on the telephone only," Leo Bloch said. "My father started me and my brother, George, in the business and George's son, Dennis, is still in there, and my daughter's husband, Joel Richards, runs the new steel division, with a general oversight of the whole

operation. It gives me an interest in living, and it's important to live. I don't know how much longer I'll have a reason. I just keep working."

Morris Bloch used to drive the countryside in a Model T truck, picking up scrap or delivering parts to logging camps, accompanied by Leo. Today, huge trucks whiz in and out delivering materials to the company's spacious salvage yard that hasn't changed much at all. A new crane slides up and down rail spurs, dumping metal items in containers, while an old cable crane does the same job in much more labored fashion nearby, with everything carted over to nearby Nucor Steel, Bloch's primary customer.

Longevity is one of Leo Bloch's strong suits, as indicated by his continued involvement in the business. But keeping it a family-run operation will be more and more challenging in the years ahead. There's only a grand-

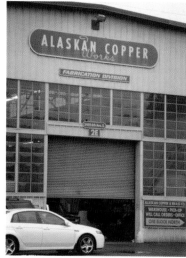

Modern-day image of one of Alaskan Copper Works facilities.

daughter, a college-bound Hannah Richards on full scholarship at Oxford, to carry on the tradition.

"Maybe my daughter will marry someone who needs a job like me," quipped Joel Richards, who wed Leo Bloch's daughter, Nancy, and has worked 31 years for the company and is its president.

Three Loyal SoDo Employees

People weren't out of line if they told Al Aurilio he was older than dirt. When it came to SoDo's filled-in tideflats, often it was true.

Aurilio was 88 when he died in 2009, not long after leaving his job of 62 years as a warehouse supervisor at Pacific Iron and Metal Company.

"He retired reluctantly because of health issues," said Doug Glant, Pacific Iron and Metal chief executive officer. "I was three years old when he started working for us. We used to talk about old unions, old employees and old customers."

Photos of a young and older Al Aurilio.

Aurilio remains the most extreme case of the loyal SoDo working man, a group of industrial-area workaholics that also includes Henry Castle, formerly a crane mechanic for Star Machinery, and Ray Gorynski, a retired Alaskan Copper Works coppersmith.

A World War II veteran, Aurilio joined Pacific Iron and Metal shortly after returning to the states from Japan. He made $1.05 per hour when he first started. He had every intention of retiring at 65, but his wife, Louise, died two years before that landmark birthday. He received an anniversary cake from his employer and kept working. He was still pulling four 5-to-11 a.m. shifts weekly during his last year on the job.

Castle was another war vet looking for work when he signed on with Star Machinery in 1946. He stayed there 42 years. It was the only job the Mississippi native ever had. A crane repairman, he was good at what he did. He was a noted character who always made his extra dangerous job look easy.

"He'd climb up and shimmy out the underside of the boom," Star Rentals co-owner Bill Rabel said. "He'd be on First Hill and see a nurse looking out the window with eyes aghast. He'd always wave, always flirt with the women. He couldn't stop doing it, even when upside down, 100 feet in the air."

Castle had one close call. Working outside of Harborview Medical Center, he was standing on a platform 40 feet in the air stringing crane cable, when everything gave way and crashed to the ground. He was able to jump onto a ledge on the first floor, avoiding serious injury or death.

"The crane demolished two automobiles," Castle said. "Everybody down there was running around, looking for me. I hollered down to them where I was. In 25 years of climbing up cranes that was the closest call I had."

When he retired in 1988, Castle was handed a piece of string at work. It led out of the office downstairs, through a shop and into a back alley, where it was tied to a new Ford Ranger pickup truck. The Skyway resident drove it until a few years ago when his retirement gift – ironically – met a SoDo demise. Castle was turning on Airport Way South when a cab driver turned into him and totaled the truck.

Safety regulations hardly were restrictive during the time that Castle worked. He was often alone when he could have used a companion to ensure his safety. He paid a physical price for the work he did, later needing multiple surgeries on his limbs.

"Star got out of the Crane business and I guess they did because I refused to climb up anymore," he said. "My knees and shoulders bothered me. You climb up cranes seven or eight times per day, with tools hanging on you, and I guess it wears on you."

An Alaskan Copper Works employee from 1939 to 1964, Gorynski didn't put in

Henry Castle and his "happy retirement cake" at Star Rentals after 42 years. He was 62 at the time.

(continued on page 20)

SoDo's Copper & Brass Connection

Alaskan Copper Works and the Alaskan Copper and Brass Company, founded by Lithuanian immigrant Morris Rosen, fill up several parcels of land on 6th Avenue South. The yellow-and-red buildings make and sell various metal products on both sides of the busy thoroughfare that runs north and south through SoDo. With 40 acres, counting properties located on neighboring streets, including a huge warehouse that sits next door to M. Bloch Company on South Colorado Street, this family-run operation ranks as the third-largest landowner in the area, behind the Port of Seattle and developer Henry Liebman. Yet 6th Avenue South remains Alaskan Copper's chief domain.

"I told them they should charge us a toll for driving across their road," joked Dave Ederer, whose deep-rooted SoDo family is well acquainted with the Rosens. "It should be Rosen Avenue."

Morris Rosen got the family business started in Seattle in 1913 by opening a coppersmith steam shop on the waterfront, moving in next door to Skinner and Eddy Shipyard. The ship builders landed a huge contract to create a fleet of English ships for World War I, and Rosen proved a ready opportunist, receiving the subcontracts that came along with it. Before long he had expanded the shop to 50 people because there was so much work coming his way.

The business would later move to 1st Avenue South, before creating an industrial beachhead on 6th Avenue South in the 1950s and expanding elsewhere. Along the way, the Alaskan Copper name became a familiar brand, with the name gleaned from Seattle's prosperous northern connections.

"My grandfather thought it was topical, coming just after the Gold Rush," said Bill Rosen, Alaskan Copper chairman and chief executive

Current image of Amick Metal Fabricators, Inc.

officer, and Morris Rosen's grandson. "It was like Miami and tropical."

Needing more space for its wholesale business, Alaskan Copper and Brass Company will relocate to leased warehouse space in Renton in 2010. The rest of the business, the manufacturing end, will remain in SoDo.

While other businesses come and go in SoDo at a rapid turnover rate, with most of the oldest fabricat-

ing shops having completely disappeared, Alaskan Copper Works maintains a steady, family-owned presence in the neighborhood. Now employing a fifth generation of Rosens, that won't change anytime soon.

"We have no other strategy," Bill Rosen said humorously. "Only a certain amount of people want to work in a business like this. It's not impossible to keep it as a family business. They are

(continued from page 18)

nearly the years on the job that Aurilio and Castle did. Or did he?

There were shifts that wouldn't end, continuously running over back-to-back days, holed up in some boiler room somewhere. There regularly were 16-hour foundry shifts that lasted until midnight.

"Sometimes I worked two days and never went home," said Gorynski, now living in Sequim. "I once worked 24 hours a day for two days in a row on a ship."

He joined Alaskan Copper as an apprentice coppersmith, earning 62-and-a-half cents per hour, and worked his way up to be the best at what he did. "He became a craftsman," said Bill Rosen, Alaskan Copper Works president. "He was a terrific metal worker."

Gorynski can remember grueling, sweaty jobs that required him pulling on a gas torch for hours, surrounded by two workers swinging away with sledgehammers, with everyone together attempting to bend a section of pipe that was 16 inches in diameter and 30 feet long. Creative breaks were offered.

"They said, 'Go across the street to the Brass Tavern and cool off, but have just one beer and come back,'" he recalled.

He remembers working on secretive war-time jobs in which he had to pass clearance checks, and he arrived at work sites that were surrounded by curtains. He fixed ship condensers, sleeping on board and eating in the captain's quarters until he was done. He helped install all of the piping at the Rainier Brewery.

Gorynski's career was saluted with a retirement party at a Lake Union restaurant, and he was given a plaque and something he didn't own at the time – a TV set.

He never complained about working or about going nonstop. He went to work for Alaskan Copper at the end of the Great Depression. He saw trains stop in the SoDo district and 1,000 men disembark, all looking for a regular paycheck. He greatly valued his job.

"Even at Alaskan Copper, if a guy didn't like you, there would be three or four guys waiting for your job, always on call," Goryinski said.

your relatives. You can't kill them. You can't fire them. We have reunions, and we remind everybody we're part of the lucky gene machine."

An Amick-able Trade

Amick Metal Fabricators is a two-story building full of broken windows, a bent readerboard and cracks in its dirty green exterior. Located at 2727 6th Avenue South, this place won't win any architectural awards, but it's still functional.

Hal Amick Sr., a transplanted Indiana man who had tired of the Midwest humidity, started this SoDo business in 1916 on Railroad Avenue, now Alaskan Way. The company's first big job was installing a heat ventilator in the Orpheum Theater. Amick died a dozen years after opening the waterfront shop, forcing his wife, Nell, to run the place in an era that didn't exactly welcome women into the workplace, especially when holding down a management position in heavy industry.

Yet she proved to be a liberated and popular employer, taking no salary through the worst of the Great Depression in order to pay her workers during tough times. Her three sons, Donald, Ed and Bob, would follow her into the business, either as management or working in the shop, and purchase the company from her.

Amick died a dozen years after opening the waterfront shop, forcing his wife, Nell, to run the place in an era that didn't exactly welcome women into the workplace, especially when holding down a management position in heavy industry.

Giving way to World War II concerns near the waterfront, Amick Metal moved to its current site in 1941 and kept busy answering urgent military needs. One of the shop's claims to fame was using the first break-presser west of the Mississippi River, a contraption that bends steel and, for its uniqueness, brought in steady work.

During the war Amick Metal cut up sheet panels that were sent to Alaska for unspecified needs, learning much later that these pieces likely were used in the hurried construction of the military's early-detection systems placed across that state and Canada. Another job had Amick working in tandem with a local shipyard on the production of all barges that would be hauling wartime goods to Alaska.

"The boatyard had the allocation sent here for cutting and forming," said current owner Hal Amick, a grandson and namesake of the founder. "We were kind of proud of that."

As a sign of slower modern times, this once bustling union shop, which

doubled its manpower to 40-plus employees during World War II, now has the younger Hal Amick and his daughter Sarah working alone in the upstairs office while a solitary boilermaker, Bill Groves, pounds away on metal orders in the shop. There haven't been too many upgrades. "All of the equipment is from the 1940s and 1950s," Groves said.

Plain Jane Plant Had Celebrities Calling

Pacific Iron and Metal likewise isn't pretty. Established by Latvian immigrant Jules Glant on 1st Avenue South in 1917 and moved to its current location at 2230 4th Avenue South 14 years later, this multi-purpose recycling company still deals with metal scrap processing in the basement, on the main floor and in an outside yard, and handles fabrics on the top floor.

It's been a hard-working place for the common man all these years, though frequent

The Glants of Pacific Iron and Metal at their other business, Pacific Fabrics, in 1968. From left to right: Earle, Jules, Bruce, Doug and Gary.

celebrity sightings also have been part of its legacy. Entertainer Jack Benny, a Glant cousin, visited the plant, as did his show-business peers Sammy Davis Jr. and Phil Harris. Countless athletes, particularly University of Washington football players, have held jobs there, though some, such as D'Marco Farr, now a TV personality, didn't always show up when required. A huge party was

thrown on the site in 1975 to welcome new Huskies coach Don James, drawing a "Who's Who" of Seattle dignitaries.

"It really hasn't changed much," said Doug Glant, chairman and chief executive officer, successor to his father Earle Glant and the grandson of Jules Glant. "We have the original building, original ceilings and original floors on this site. My board of directors comes in here and

Earle Glant, grandson of founder Jules Glant, in the yard at Pacific Iron and Metal.

has been at the same site since the height of the Great Depression and moving it to another place. It will remain business as usual, just the way Jules Glant started it.

"We have a creaky old building," Doug Glant said. "We repair it when it needs it. I'd rather pay the employees and myself than move and build another one."

says, 'Doug, it's like walking into the past.' "

The Glants mostly sell their recycled metals overseas, to China and Korea, while collecting scrap materials from Alaska by container ship, Eastern Washington by outside trucks and locally by their own trucks.

After adding a home sewing business in the late 1950s, a product line since discontinued, Pacific Iron and Metal once had Seattle women lined up around the block, festively waiting to purchase bargain swimsuits that were offered three for $10.

This was a yearly sale held more for promotional means, creating a scene that hardly matched the gritty industrial surroundings. More typical were visits by the unlimited hydroplane racing crews who prowled around the yard looking through the accumulated stuff for engine parts.

While Doug Glant concedes it doesn't make sense today to have a scrap yard operating not much more than a mile from Seattle's high-rises and even closer to its pro sports stadiums, he has resisted packing up this long-running operation that

"We have the original building, original ceilings and original floors on this site. My board of directors comes in here and says, 'Doug, it's like walking into the past.' "

Doug Glant

Harold Stack used to sell steel in SoDo. He worked for his father and then operated Stack Steel and Supply Company by himself. Life at the 2201 6th Avenue South fabricating plant, however, was not all about filling orders and sending out heavy shipments.

After a day of fruitless duck hunting on the Skagit flats in the 1950s, Stack showed up at the steel yard the following morning around 6 a.m. with one thing in mind. It wasn't work-related. Marshlands bordered his family-owned company to the north. A Bar S meat-packing plant feed lot for cattle headed for slaughter sat next to the pond. It all made for the perfect duck blind.

Maneuvering through the outside steel racks, an Ithaca 37 shotgun in hand, Stack rose up and peppered the sky with early Sunday morning gunfire. His Skagit skunking was now a distant memory. He scurried around and collected his urban kill.

"There were ducks coming in like you wouldn't believe," he said. "I shot my limit in a half hour or so."

After stuffing the weapon and downed fowl inside the trunk of his car, Stack was getting ready to head home when a Seattle police officer drove up. The cop explained there had been numerous complaints phoned in by Beacon Hill residents about someone shooting a gun in the area below their homes, and he wanted to know if the steel executive had seen anything suspicious.

The law enforcement official received only shrugs. "I said I had just got there and was getting stuff in my office," Stack said. "I wasn't going to admit to getting a

Maneuvering through the outside steel racks, an Ithaca 37 shotgun in hand, Stack rose up and peppered the sky with early Sunday morning gunfire. His Skagit skunking was now a distant memory. He scurried around and collected his urban kill.

limit of ducks in the middle of the city."

While half of SoDo's tidelands were filled in methodically, creating a new ground surface that ran from the waterfront to 4th Avenue South, the inner half of the industrial district to Beacon Hill still had plenty of vacant spaces and liquid-like obstacles that remained that way through the Eisenhower presidency. Most SoDo buildings still had to be constructed on stilts or pilings. Though it wasn't recommended, business owners like Harold Stack for the longest time could

come and go on safari, undetected in the shadows of the Seattle skyline.

"It was pretty primitive down there," he said. "Sears and Roebuck was the main building, and there wasn't much else."

A Tower in the Swamp

There was no hiding the Sears and Roebuck Company in the barren cat-tail reeds of SoDo. It stuck out like a huge freighter on a small pond. This Chicago-based mail-order company turned up in Seattle in 1910, in a small temporary sales office in Pioneer Square, the first for the company outside of Illinois. Almost overnight, the catalog business made a full retreat to Seattle's newly-filled-in industrial district, its headquarters rising out of the ground in sections, fueled by ridiculous growth.

By 1912, Sears and Roebuck had built a functional yet mundane six-story building at 2401 Utah Avenue South on leased

The Sears Building, shortly after it was constructed.

railroad land. Three years later, after renting out seven more storage areas to service its accelerated warehousing needs, the company turned more creative with architectural demands to further its expansion. It erected a nine-floor building complete with a trademark clock tower, a structure that lords over this Seattle business district today. Horse-and-buggy shops lined 1st Avenue South opposite the new structure, and a railway spur ran through the first floor of the rapidly expanding building.

In five rapid-fire years, from opening its doors uptown to unveiling its beacon-like facility in SoDo, Sears and Roebuck went from 25,000 square feet of floor space, seven employees and $320,000 in earnings to an entire square block of storefront, roughly 1,000 people on the company payroll and an incredible $8.5 million in yearly revenue. The catalog business was wildly popular with customers throughout the West Coast, cutting out the greedy middle man and reducing needless cost. People in Seattle didn't have to wait long to receive their orders, either.

"We were located across the street from Sears and I remember ordering my first baseball glove," said Ernie Sherman, whose family founded Sherman Supply Company near Sears and Roebuck and who owns Pacific Plumbing Supply Company, with both businesses now in Georgetown. "I bought it mail order, paid for it at the desk, and came back three or four hours later and picked it up."

Shirley Morrison grew up as a Sears and Roebuck customer and worked for the company from 1964 to 1989, originally in a parts and service warehouse at 4786 1st Avenue South. Her employee discount of 10 to 15 percent on merchandise came in handy in meeting her growing family's needs, both in picking up a new refrigerator and oven and taking care of holiday shopping.

"I had three children and it was a very big thing for

them," Morrison said. "When the Christmas catalog would come out, they would look through it until it was worn out, picking out what they wanted."

In time, Seattle's Sears and Roebuck flagship store would become so big, with 1.8 million square feet on one site and a payroll of 3,400, it was considered the largest building of its kind on the West Coast. It remains the second-biggest building of any kind in the Puget Sound region in modern times, surpassed only by Boeing's jet assembly plant in Everett.

Henry Bowers, a Michigan man assigned to find a western location for Sears and Roebuck, hand-picked

It remains the second-biggest building of any kind in the Puget Sound region in modern times, surpassed only by Boeing's jet assembly plant in Everett.

Seattle. He served as the local store general manager until 1933, when poor health forced him to retire. He remained in the Northwest, living in Bellingham, until his death in 1966. After likely working way too much in making the Seattle outlet a huge company success, not working had its benefits, too. He was 95 when he passed away.

The Great Depression hardly slowed business, with 869 local Sears and Roebuck workers contributing a day's pay for unemployment relief while their employer matched these funds. Company mergers with J.C. Penney and Montgomery Ward were considered and ultimately rejected. In 1940, Sears and Roebuck, still thinking big, announced plans to build an automotive service center near the catalog business. Up to 300 cars could be parked and worked on while owners went across the street and shopped.

Almost as Big as the Bible, then Changes Come

At one point, the Sears and Roebuck catalog was said to have greater distribution nationwide than any other book except the Bible. Yet into the 1980s, this customer service-oriented business would grow obsolete, with the emergence of self-service outlets such as Costco becoming the cheaper alternative to what had once served as the cheap alternative. Sears and Roebuck would be forced to shut down its Seattle catalog center in 1987, sending the remnants of the business to Los Angeles, opening a new distribution center in Reno and putting the once-bustling SoDo building up for sale. The company would maintain retail store outlets throughout the region and the auto-repair service shop still exists near the original store, but the boom days were effectively over.

"They just kind of reduced it in size and I'm not sure

An invoice is kept tucked away in the shop, demonstrating progress. The date on this yellowed piece of paper is December 22, 1933. The bill is for $791.40 from the W.L. Feely Company to cover 20,000 board feet of Douglas fir lumber. "That would be like $75,000 now."

Kevin Cochrane

whose idea it was to do that," Morrison said. "It was a good place to work. We did a lot of good business. But at the end it was not nearly as good as it used to be."

New Neighbors Come In

While corporate-minded Sears and Roebuck Company towered over SoDo, a second wave of family-owned businesses gained a foothold and lasted as long as the mail-order giant, or outlasted it.

Warren Cochrane in his office in September 1939, and later on in life.

Exterior of Millwork Supply circa 1930s and inside the company in 2009.

Among them were Stack Steel and Supply, Millwork Supply, Robinson Machine and Gear Works, Sherman Supply, Systems Transfer and Storage, and Lee and Eastes Tank Lines.

SoDo grew into an intricate grid of crisscrossing streets, not yet encumbered by trains and bus lanes.

Seattle Boulevard was renamed Airport Way. Railroad Avenue was changed to Alaskan Way. Trolleys rolled up and down 1st Avenue South until 1941. 6th Avenue South was built wider than most SoDo streets to facilitate truck traffic.

Millwork Supply at 2225 1st

Avenue South opened in 1924 and, a year later, Warren A. Cochrane was sent by a Yakima shareholder to shut it down, with people under the mistaken impression the company wasn't doing well. Cochrane not only didn't close the place, he eventually bought up all of the company shares

from creditors who were encouraged to assume the roles of stockholders. In 1985, he finally retired at 89, stepping away from a business that had given him a paycheck for more than six decades and has now employed four generations of his family, and is still doing a good business despite those early forecasts to the contrary.

A wooden sign commemorating Cochrane's 60th anniversary on the job was cut in the shop and hung up in the office. The sign was reused a few years later, with the six turned upside down when this tireless man celebrated his 90th birthday.

Cochrane was succeeded by his son, Warren D. Cochrane, who likewise retired after nearly 60 years on the job and gave way to his sons, John and Kevin, and daughter, Cori. John's and Kevin's daughters, Caitlin and Shaina, respectively, have pulled shifts in the shop or as janitors, keeping the family's Millwork Supply connection alive.

"We've been really, really

SoDo's OK Lunch

The OK Lunch was a brown shack of a building at 510 West Spokane Street, a place with uneven wood floors, leaky roof, sagging ceiling, no telephone, no heat and 10 exposed light bulbs.

Behind the "U-shaped" counter serving customers occupying 40 stools, sisters Minnie Ireland, Myrtle Reis and Mabel Hansen were feisty and impatient. They never wrote anything down. They hollered orders to the cook. They expressed displeasure with those who couldn't decide. They always knew the bill in their heads. They were a Saturday Night Live skit forever waiting to happen.

"It was a serious, raucous caucus," Bill Rosen, Alaskan Copper Works president and OK Lunch regular, said poetically.

Truckers, longshoremen and other members of SoDo's mostly working class jammed into this place to consume the home-cooked special of the day, leftovers from the previous special of the day or a hamburger, with pie for dessert. The busy eatery, not much bigger than a logging camp cookhouse, opened at 4:30 a.m. and closed at 2 p.m.

"My dad and I ate there every day for decades," said Warren D. Cochrane, referring to the late Warren A. Cochrane, two generations of Millwork Supply owners.

"It wasn't a very fancy place," said Don Morrison, former Fisher Flour Company grain elevator operator. "It was a worker's cafeteria, you might say. It sure was good."

A blackboard served as the menu, cigar boxes and muffin tins as the cash register. A steaming plate of roast beef, mashed potatoes and gravy, and green beans fetched $2.20. A cheeseburger deluxe cost $1. Soup was 50 cents. Scones filled with butter and strawberry jam were made on Wednesdays and went for 40 cents.

Didn't want a full order? "A baby meatloaf for Warren!" was yelled back to the cook, describing the reduced portion.

One of the sisters habitually used to tabulate bills on the tips of her fingers, leading someone to hang five old gloves from the ceiling below a sign that read, "Myrt's Lightning Calculator – Pat. Pending."

On occasion the sisters used to roll dice with customers, double or nothing to settle the bill. They won 90 percent of the time. No one questioned the odds of this. If a sister dropped and broke a plate, the others would paddle her on the back side to everyone's delight.

Wedged between a scrap yard and warehouse and across the street from the Brass Tavern, the OK Lunch opened in 1918. Five different women, all related in some manner, were the proprietors.

The popular diner shut its doors for good in 1980, giving way to progress when West Seattle Freeway expansion eliminated many of the businesses located at or near the corner of West Spokane Street and East Marginal Way.

"We'd always go to a late lunch," Warren D. Cochrane said. "We'd always carry the garbage out for them when we left. It was sad, but someone took a picture on the last day when they saw my dad turn the sign over from 'Open' to 'Closed.' "

lucky because we had personalities that all worked well together," John Cochrane said. "There was a job here for us, and over time that job became a career."

The business has survived earthquakes, economic downturns and all sorts of modern change. Old company photos from the 1930s hang prominently in the lobby, preserving memories. An invoice is kept tucked away in the shop, demonstrating progress. The date on this yellowed piece of paper is December 22, 1933. The bill is for $791.40 from the W.L. Feely Company to cover 20,000 board feet of Douglas fir lumber.

"That would be like $75,000 now," Kevin Cochrane pointed out.

Tough Guy Keeps Unions at Bay

The brick-faced building at 2915 1st Avenue South, which is located a couple of blocks south of Millwork Supply on the same side of the same street, was built and owned

Contemporary view of Snoqualmie Falls, east of Seattle. The turbines used here were aided by the gears built by SoDo's Robinson Gear and Machine Works.

by the Robinson family from 1929 to 2008, which was ironically buffered by economic downturns at each end.

On this site, Joseph Robinson founded Robinson Gear and Machine Works, a company that designed, built and repaired precision gears, with his work most prominently used in the running of the Snoqualmie Falls power turbines. Robinson was a determined man, a Pennsylvanian who overcame a West Virginia mine collapse and, after four days of underground confinement, insisted he would die first before submitting to amputation of both hands crushed by falling timber in the accident. That mine collapse is said to have turned his hair white.

Operating a non-union shop, Robinson received threats from union members who strongly suggested he consider changing his employment practice. He proceeded to hang paper rifle targets from the ceiling that displayed bulls-eye accuracy. He pointed them out the next time the strong-armed types returned to his shop. He failed to mention that the targets belonged to his daughter, who was a member of the University of Washington rifle team that often competed nationally. The union goons never returned.

After Robinson's death in 1949, that same daughter, Margery Phillips, leased the building to various tenants until recently selling off the SoDo property. The irreverent Year of the Monkey, an import business that sells Asian home furnishings and is run by a man named Hunter Marshall, now occupies the address.

> *Robinson received threats from union members who strongly suggested he consider changing his employment practice. He hung paper rifle targets from the ceiling that displayed bulls-eye accuracy and pointed them out the next time the strong-armed types returned to his shop. He failed to mention that the targets belonged to his daughter, who was a member of the University of Washington rifle team that often competed nationally. The union goons never returned.*

Russian Czar Sends Businessman to SoDo

SoDo can thank the Russian Army of the early 1900s for Sherman Supply. Abe Sherman was a Polish teenager facing involuntary service to the Czar when he followed his mother's advice and left for America. He took the long way to reach the Northwest, making stops in Paris and New York.

Sherman encouraged his brothers to join him from Europe and become scrap dealers in Seattle. They conducted business out of a section of an old warehouse at 917 1st Avenue South, a building that was demolished in 2009 as preparations were made for the construction of the city's new waterfront tunnel.

"I was a little kid about seven and my dad would take me down to the original Sherman Supply, and we'd walk a couple of blocks and fish off the piers," Ernie Sherman recalled.

At the completion of World War II, Sherman Supply moved to 2456 1st Avenue South and stayed at that SoDo site for the next six decades, until the 2001 Nisqually earthquake damaged much of the place – a week after the business had been remodeled. Morris Sherman, Ernie's father, would break off from his brothers and open Pacific Supply Company, a comparable business that set up shop at a nearby SoDo location, 1500 1st Avenue South.

"That was sort of a hub for plumbing supply," Ernie Sherman said of that particu-

The four Sherman brothers who created their eponymous supply company (from left to right): Abe, Maurice, Jack and Luigi Sherman.

lar 1st Avenue South corridor. "A lot of them got their start as scrap dealers."

Among its biggest jobs, Sherman Supply provided many of the hose pipes and fittings for the Alaskan oil pipeline. The business moved to Georgetown after the city forced family members to give

The first door lock and a horseshoe manufactured at Stack Steel's original 1932 plant.

up the 1st Avenue South site – citing light-rail imminent domain, a project that never materialized on that street, which was a source of great frustration for Abe Sherman's descendents.

There were four Sherman brothers in all, with trailblazing Abe convincing younger siblings Morris, Jack and Louis to join him. All of these men were ambitious, though not necessarily in the same manner. Sherman Supply carried everyone through the Great Depression. However, by 1933

Louis Sherman would become Luigi DeSilva and a headline opera singer, debuting at the Milan Opera House and later performing in New York.

Idea Man from Iowa

George Eastes was a young man full of ambition, a truck driver who kept coming up with ideas for the local company that employed him. His exasperated boss informed the eager 22-year-old from Burlington, Iowa, that he should open his own business.

In 1923, Eastes did just that, breaking off with fellow driver, Art Lee, to form a trucking company originally located midway between Seattle and Puyallup.

Three years later, Lee and Eastes moved into SoDo, expanding the 1016 Airport Way South terminal into one of the West Coast's leading trucking lines. At its peak, the company was running 90 trucks. It would move to its current location at 2418 Airport Way South, where dispatch offices are still situated and three bays perform truck repairs. The tankers typically haul gasoline, diesel or liquid asphalt.

Four generations of family members have been involved with Lee and Eastes. Founder George J. Eastes coaxed his father, George V. Eastes, to leave Illinois and join him as a company accountant. He next turned the business over to his son, Gary Eastes, who remains as chairman. A granddaughter, Jill Newcomb, is company president. A grandson, Bruce Eastes, formerly worked as a Lee and Eastes journeyman mechanic and shop manager before becoming a SoDo real-estate developer, with his office now adjoining the trucking company.

"Dad thought he knew

Lee & Eastes double-trailer truck circa 1948.

Rainier Brewery

The beer taps were shut off over a decade ago. The building now serves coffee of all things and the most famous "R" in Seattle sits in a museum, yet the Rainier Brewery is visible for all to see, a SoDo reference point no less. Parts of the former brewery quite possibly qualify as the industrial district's oldest remaining structures, dating as far back as 1885. In his unpublished memoir, the late Emil Sick described in 1933 how he tore down everything except the walls while remodeling the building at 3100 Airport Way South. It originally served as the Bayview Brewery but was converted to a feed mill before returning to its original use by Sick.

"It was only 15 minutes driving time from the heart of the city," Sick said, explaining the property acquisition. "It was up on the bank of the hill at some elevation, whereas much of the land further west is 'made' land, formerly tideflats. My father did not think much of tideflats as a building foundation."

Sick, who died in 1964, would turn the place into an empire, making Rainier the city's most popular alcoholic beverage as well as the nickname of the local professional baseball team, the Seattle Rainiers, which Sick also owned. The brewery's popular sampling room offered free schooners to visitors, with the Western Washington University rugby team from Bellingham always taking full advantage and making this place a regular part of its itineraries on southern road trips, sometimes to the point these college kids had to be gently urged to move on.

Today, the building is the more sedate home to Tully's Coffee, with its green "T" replacing the Rainier "R," plus artist lofts, storage units and assorted small businesses. Trying to maintain past connections, a sign was recently erected that also identifies the place as "the Old Rainier Brewery." A green statue of a female, described as the "Spirit of Good Living" and supposedly imported from Germany in 1903, remains in full pose on the property.

The brewery building might be SoDo's sturdiest as well as the oldest. It consists of 24 individual buildings, hung together with double walls and 14-inch-thick concrete floors. "The thing is built like a bunker," Tully's owner Tom "Tully" O'Keefe said. "If there's an earthquake, come here."

The Old Rainier Brewery came to life when Prohibition was repealed, and was operated by the Sick family from 1934 to 1977. The business later was sold, in succession, to Heileman, Stroh's and Pabst breweries, operating as a beer-maker through 1999 before changing to a more caffeinated course.

The original Rainier Brewery

everything and he told (employer) Asal Strain why don't you do this and do that?" Gary Eastes said. "Asal finally said, 'Damn it, George, if you're so smart, why don't you start your own truck line?' The rest is history."

More Truckers Move In

System Transfer and Storage is another family-run trucking company, with 54 of its 90 years of service coming in the SoDo District after previous business locations on Beacon Hill and in Belltown.

In 1956, Lloyd Coder opened a new facility at 2400 6th Avenue South, encouraged to go where the land was cheap and there was lots of it. The property was former tideland before the trucks arrived. The building had to be erected on pilings because of soil instability and it shook when trains zipped past. It once had access for 12 rail cars.

Through the years the company has delivered metal fabricating, air conditioning units, delicatessen counters and products for Starbucks and Tully's coffee companies throughout the city.

Coder's grandsons, Stewart and Scott Soules, run the business, which includes a huge warehouse for storage. There's always been a strong push to keep it in the family.

"Our grandfather worked here until he died in 1971," Scott Soules pointed out. "A lot of people went out of here feet first."

Scrap Scion Grows Family Business into Real Estate Empire

Stack Steel and Salvage Company officially was founded in 1932 by German immigrant Eugene Stack, evolving from a business started 20 years earlier in a little shed next to what would become the Sears and Roebuck site. Stack's modest operation sat on rented property at the corner of Utah Avenue South

"I've seen a lot of changes. I've seen a place where you could shoot ducks go to a place full of solid buildings."

Harold Stack

and South Stacy Street, space now used for a multi-tiered parking garage. Stack drove a truck around town and collected recyclable materials, turning his resourcefulness into an empire.

"My grandfather never let a scrap of metal go to waste," said Robb Stack, a third-generation family member.

By 1946, Eugene Stack had done well enough that he purchased a tideflat lot and built a steel fabricating plant at 2201 6th Avenue South, next to that prime duck-hunting marsh. The business would flourish for the next three decades, eventually expanding its manufacturing operations to Spokane, Portland and Anchorage behind

the leadership of his son, Harold Stack. The Stack family would sell the steel company at its peak and then reclaim the property after the new owners ran into serious financial difficulties. They would close the plant in 1984 but hang onto the land.

Following the advice of his father, Robb Stack leases out but doesn't sell the family's considerable SoDo real estate holdings, outside of the large chunk of property that was purchased by the city, citing imminent domain for the new light-rail train system that began operations in the summer of 2009. The company roots are never far away. In his office, the younger Stack keeps the first door lock and a horseshoe from the original 1932 steel plant displayed in a picture frame.

He acknowledges that change in SoDo has taken place. "It's not just a pure industrial district that it once was," said Robb Stack, who worked briefly for the family steel company. "The neighborhood is changing. We've got light rail and Costco. We've got a lot of things that make this part of town look more urban than industrial. There's a real mixed bag of stuff here."

Harold Stack remembers the family paying a dollar a square foot for the steel plant land and says the property is now worth nearly 20 times that. He remembers when Sixth Avenue South was a dirt road, and paved not long after his memorable duck-hunting expedition, giving into modernization if not negating his sporting pursuits. He has never forgotten four and a half years of serious haggling with the city over the land that was reclaimed, stubbornly making sure his family members were overcompensated for the property if it had to be handed over.

"I told my kids to buy land and hold it," Harold Stack pointed out. "It's the one thing this world isn't making anymore. You've got a limited supply for a great demand. I'm 93 and probably one of the older owners of real estate still alive. I've seen a lot of changes. I've seen a place where you could shoot ducks go to a place full of solid buildings."

Waterfront homes turned up practically overnight in Seattle, offering fabulous views of the city skyline and Elliott Bay. Yet there were no high-priced architects or fast-talking realtors hovering about. There were no million-dollar man-

> *There were no million-dollar mansions or glitzy condominiums with all the trappings. Luxury involved a whiff of the briny saltwater, little more. People were trying to move out, not move in.*

sions or glitzy condominiums with all the trappings. Luxury involved a whiff of the briny saltwater, little more. People were trying to move out, not move in.

From 1931 to 1941, Seattle's Hooverville was a sprawling homeless encampment at harbor's edge that was created in the aftermath of the Great Depression. It carried an identifying tag shared by similar shelters nationwide, one mocking a previous American president who had proved powerless to prevent the numbing economic disaster. In this case, as many as 1,100 people huddled together in the abandoned Skinner and Eddy Shipyard, most of them men occupying crudely built shacks or sleeping in tents, all victims of extremely lean times.

Developers today are doing everything thing they can to bring residential housing to SoDo, especially perched along the waterfront, only to have strict zoning restrictions prevent anything of that sort

from happening. Yet there was a time when people actually slept close enough to the harbor's edge to watch the tide go in and out and to soak in this now sacred ground. The truth was, no one really wanted to live there.

Tough Times Lead to Ingenuity & Survival

This was a Spartan town within a seaport city, located in what has become north SoDo. It was a predecessor

When Art Mendelsohn was 10, he often cut through Hooverville to go fishing off the end of King Street.

> *"I used to walk among those people. They were no different than you or I. They were good people who just needed jobs. They wanted to work."*
>
> Art Mendelsohn

to the modern-day Port of Seattle ship-container yard that now sits on this priceless property and is located two blocks west of a glistening playground that was built for baseball and football millionaires, Safeco Field and Qwest Field. Could two worlds turn out at more opposite ends of the spectrum than this? Luckless souls taking over the old shipyard site and erecting makeshift wood and tin shacks on top of tideland fill was a deliberate act of desperation. They had no place to go.

"I used to walk among those people," said Art Mendelsohn, a former SoDo business owner, who, when he was

10, would boldly cut through Hooverville to go fishing off the end of King Street. "They were no different than you or I. They were good people who just needed jobs. They wanted to work."

Hooverville was a name coined by Charles Mickelson, no less the national press secretary for the Democratic Party. He couldn't pass up taking an opportunistic jab at President Herbert Hoover, a Republican who while in office watched the 1929 Stock Market Crash send the country into a crippling economic spiral.

Thirteen million people, or a quarter of the entire U.S. work force, were left without jobs. In Seattle, it was reported at one time that 22,104 people lived in various Hoovervilles around the city, also called Shacktowns or Shantytowns, with most emerging in or around what is now considered SoDo. Other sites included Beacon Hill, Harbor Island, the Sears property and an inactive Washington Iron

Hooverville during its heydays in the 1930s.

Works plant. Elsewhere in the city, Interbay, the banks of the Duwamish River and various industrial parks, railroad yards and tidelands also offered homeless refuges.

The Skinner and Eddy Shipyard was the most visible gathering place for those struggling to exist because of its proximity: It was situated next door to solvent downtown Seattle and big business. Three years after the Wall Street crash, word spread around town that this waterfront site was unused and full of a large amount of discarded lumber that could be used for building shelters and burning heat. Anxious people gravitated there in droves. The city tried to discourage the makeshift living arrangement, with authorities razing more than three dozen shacks and chasing off everyone, only to

Plane Crashes in SoDo

One military airplane didn't make it back to Boeing Field, another didn't survive takeoff. Their test runs went horrifically wrong. Eight years and a mile apart, these ill-fated flights crashed near the same street in SoDo, leaving woeful scenes of death and destruction.

On February 18, 1943, with the U.S. fully engaged in World War II, a B-29 bomber caught on fire as it circled over the region and nosedived into the Frye meat-packing plant at 2203 Airport Way South.

On February 18, 1943, with the U.S. fully engaged in World War II, a B-29 bomber caught on fire as it circled over the region and nosedived into the Frye meat-packing plant at 2203 Airport Way South on its return, killing 32 people in the plane and on the ground – marking Seattle's worst-ever aviation accident.

Experiencing engine trouble as it left Boeing Field on August 13, 1951, a B-50 Superfortress struggled to gain altitude and struck Sick's Rainier Brewery at 3100 Airport Way South before cartwheeling into the neighboring Lester Apartments, killing 11 people altogether.

"We heard it crash," said Harold Stack, working at the family-owned Stack Steel at the time of the second deadly flight. "We got right over there after it happened. The police were already there."

SoDo has experienced its fair share of death and fire, but nothing has proven more sensational for the industrial district than these two plane crashes.

The B-29 wasn't in the air more than 20 minutes when one of its four engines burst into flames. A wing became fully engulfed by fire. Smoke billowed from the plane. Pilot Eddie Allen and his crew of 10 urgently tried to land to the south at Boeing Field, but came up three miles short. Just after noon, the plane dropped on top of the Frye plant and exploded.

Twenty meat-packing workers on the ground were killed, as were 80 animals headed for slaughter. Two of the airmen died when their parachutes didn't open after jumping from the plane. A firefighter was killed by an ammonia release at the site. The city experienced a significant power outage.

While the military closed off the scene and wandering pigs were herded up, reporters were given no details whatsoever about the type of aircraft, or provided any information since it was classified due to its war-time development. The B-29 actually was the second one built by Boeing and the same model that would drop atomic bombs on Japan two years later.

The Frye packing plant was gutted and would later be rebuilt and sold. Today, it houses the Washington State Toxicology Laboratory, analyzing results taken from suspected drunken drivers.

In 1951, witnesses watched the B-50 take off to the north and wobble over SoDo before it banked sharply to the right, clipped the brewery and slammed into a 49-unit apartment building at 2:15 p.m.

"It looked like it was coming right at me," said John Hayes, a Rainier Brewery worker at the time. "I dropped down and sprawled flat on my face. The plane touched the roof of the brewery, and then crashed on the apartment house."

Killed on board were three Boeing flight engineers and three airmen, including pilot Lloyd Vanderwielen. Three men and two women died inside the flattened housing complex. The plane was carrying 4,000 gallons of fuel.

A third of the Lester Apartments were destroyed, in effect erasing some of Seattle's sordid past. Home to Boeing machinists and other working-class people when the crash happened, the place previously had been a notorious bordello. The building completely disappeared when Interstate 5 was built on the property the following decade.

relent and allow these helpless people to stay once they returned.

Organizing the Squatters

Jesse Jackson, a native Texan who had worked as a logger south of Seattle before he was laid off, was elected Hooverville mayor each of the seven years he lived there before finally finding work and moving on. His politics did not follow the norm. He preferred to blame his unemployment on President Calvin Coolidge, who was replaced by Hoover.

"Now personally, I always liked Herbert Hoover," Jackson told the Seattle Post-Intelligencer. "I'd always been of the opinion that Cal Coolidge remained silent when he should have cried out, but no matter. Hooverville it was."

On muddy ground strewn with brush, people built shacks out of whatever materials they could scrounge up. Some residents grew vegeta-

Leo Lassen, the voice of the Seattle Rainiers.

bles and flowers around their residences. A wholesale bakery sent a weekly truckload of unsold or broken goods to the site. Stew meat and fish often were donated. Burn barrels kept people warm. A local business provided Hooverville with a large radio and speaker to keep everyone entertained, prompting a group of the residents to pool their money and secure electricity in order to listen to nightly Seattle Rainiers baseball games and the soothing tones of famed broadcaster Leo Lassen. It

wasn't uptown living, but it was home.

The encampment was bordered on the south by Connecticut Street (now Royal Brougham Way), on the east by Railroad Avenue (now East Marginal Way), on the north by Charles Street (with some encampment overflow stretching beyond it) and on the west by Elliott Bay. Five outhouses – one set aside for women – were mounted at the end of makeshift piers called "Rat Walks" that were elevated over the harbor. High tide

would creep within 10 feet of the nearest shack.

"It was a hodgepodge of cardboard, corrugated stuff and whatever anybody could find or steal," said Warren D. Cochrane, who rode past Hooverville on a streetcar on his way to nearby Millwork Supply, where his father worked and he would later join him on the job. "There was no organization to it. No sanitation. It was something to stay clear of. There was a certain amount of violence,

A local business provided Hooverville with a large radio and speaker to keep everyone entertained, prompting a group of the residents to pool their money and secure electricity in order to listen to nightly Seattle Rainiers baseball games and the soothing tones of famed broadcaster Leo Lassen. It wasn't uptown living, but it was home.

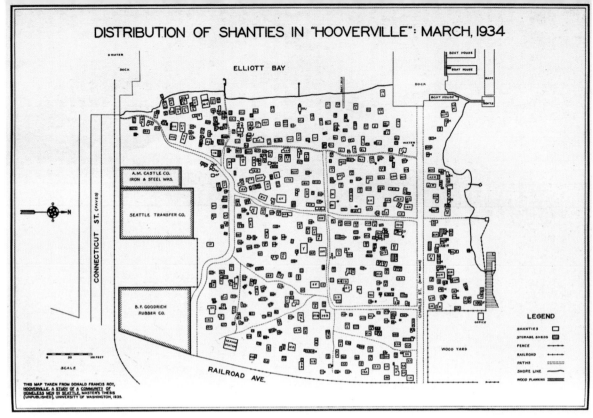

DISTRIBUTION OF SHANTIES IN "HOOVERVILLE": MARCH, 1934

Donald Roy mapped out the entire Hooverville area and assigned a number to each home, making mail delivery possible.

and I don't think it was well publicized, because it was self-policed. It was just a sprawling mess."

UW Researcher Does Hooverville Study

One of the Hooverville residents was found to be a ringer. In 1934, Donald Roy was a University of Washington student who purchased a shack for $15 for the sole purpose of living among the homeless and doing research on them for multiple recipients. One was for writing his college thesis, entitled "Hooverville, a Study of a Community of Homeless Men in Seattle." He also was hired by the Washington Emergency Relief Administration to supply that outfit with various data. He stayed two months. He slipped out daily to find a restaurant meal and occasionally seek the comfort of a clean hotel room.

Roy mapped out the entire Hooverville, tirelessly walking off distances, drawing a map of all dwellings and supplying a 12-part grid. He assigned a number to each home, making mail delivery possible, which was most important for the receipt of relief checks. In his short stay, Roy determined there were 639 residents, seven of which were women. Residents ranged in age from 18 to 73, with 45 the average, making the encampment predominantly middle-aged. Five people were college graduates. There were six married couples and no children.

Ethnically, the breakdown was as follows: 455 Caucasians, 120 Filipinos, 29 African Americans, 25 Mexicans, three Costa Ricans, two Japanese, two Native Alaskans, two Native Americans and one Chilean. There were no outward racial barriers as found elsewhere, with everyone's shared economic woes effectively bringing all races together. Of the whites, one was a former German sailor who had fought against the U.S. in World War I, his presence indicating no apparent hard feelings over previous strife between his homeland and new surroundings. Unskilled laborer, or "shovel stiff," was the listed occupation for most of these hard-luck people.

"It's pretty tough," said Hooverville resident Jack Rainier, who was 64 when he was interviewed by the Post-Intelligencer in 1941. "I've fixed up my place pretty nicely and I've been able to get by. But now I don't know. Come another year and I'll be eligible for an old-age pension. But if I can't eat for a year, I won't be alive to claim it."

Census-takers counted Hooterville residents among the city population. At one time, 750 homeless people were registered to vote in one Seattle precinct. Mayoral and city council candidates regu-

Bulldozers roared through a vacated Hooverville and flattened the shacks, shoving them into mountainous piles before bonfires reduced everything to ashes.

larly visited the encampment, chatting up the residents and campaigning for support.

No Mac-Mansions These

Most dwellings were rectangular, from 3 feet by 9 feet to 12 by 15. The largest was 15 by 25, smallest 3 by 6. One or two people occupied each place. Every shanty had a homemade stove. Some had floors made of planks. Blankets, burlap bags and anything soft were used for mattresses placed on top of wood frames. Mirrors and photos hung on the inside

An aerial view of Hooverville before the shanties were leveled.

An aerial view of Hooverville after the shanties were leveled.

walls of most. Garbage was dumped in the bay.

Some people were suspicious of Roy and all his questions, wondering out loud if he was spying on them in some sort of law-enforcement capacity. Most residents welcomed his probing efforts, even after learning of the real reasons for his presence, pleased he wasn't actually a cop. Roy was not all about empirical data, either. He was somewhat of a poet in this vivid description of Hooverville:

"From the sandy waste of an abandoned shipyard site, (Hooverville) was swiftly hammered and wired to flower a conglomerate of grotesque dwells, a Christmas-mix assortment of American junk that stuck together in congested disarray like sea-soaked jetsam spewed on the beach," Roy wrote in his UW thesis, published in 1935.

Of his own living situation, Roy claimed to have placed "a curse on the rat that gnawed under the flooring at night,"

and said he had evicted a roommate/assistant "who snored vigorously from 11 p.m. to 8 a.m." Of his leaking homemade stove, he noted that "one could smoke a winter's supply of fish."

Roy wrote that reading, card-playing, chatting and drinking were the leading encampment activities. A bottle of denatured alcohol readily was available on site for 50 cents a quart. Sadly, he concluded, "The Hooverville lacks hope."

Poverty + Booze = Crime

Newspaper reports at the time confirmed as much, showing that suicide was prevalent among Hoovervillians. One man hanged himself. Another slashed his wrists. Yet another drowned himself in the bay. There were frequent accidental deaths. Several men were killed in fires caused by stoves or lanterns tipping over. And there was the occasional murder, often fueled by excessive alcohol. One man died in a dispute over a measly quarter.

Mendelsohn, however, never once feared for his safety during his childhood fishing expeditions that took him directly through the heart of Hooverville. He found youth had its privilege among those suffering hardship. "They were kind of protective of kids," he said. "They would take it upon themselves to make sure everything was OK. They weren't criminals."

While some city officials tried to look the other way, there were repeated calls by neighborhood groups and the health department to limit or remove these illegal settlements, beginning with the highly visible Hooverville. Encroachment on private property and unsanitary conditions were the chief complaints. At the same time, these indignant and more fortunate residents didn't have any ready solutions for what to do with the people.

"Just like someone said once, we're men who are just

> *"Just like someone said once, we're men who are just shipwrecks. These little places are the planks we found to keep us afloat. And they even want to take away our planks."*
>
> Hooverville resident
> Ralph Burrows

shipwrecks," Hooverville resident Ralph Burrows told the Post-Intelligencer, explaining that he was able to survive on a $5.60 monthly relief food voucher. "These little places are the planks we found to keep us afloat. And they even want to take away our planks."

War Closes Hooverville

The prospect of World War II ultimately brought Hooverville and the citywide homeless communities to an end. With U.S. involvement in overseas fighting a certainty, local jobs were created by war needs and made available again to a wide array of people who had gone without for so long because of the Depression, allowing them to flee their shacks and find housing upgrades.

For the homeless holdouts that remained behind, the military demanded they uproot in order to reclaim the waterfront for a war-time staging area. Steamship terminals would be constructed immediately along the waterfront, preparing for battle. People would be encouraged to leave their shacks and move to suburban farm land. The Harbor Island encampment, which was nicknamed "Louisville," was the first to be dismantled in 1940 as then Todd Drydock Company, anticipating huge defense contracts coming its way, made plans for hurried expansion and asked everyone to leave. Hooverville wasn't far behind.

"My father took me down to see it before and after it was bulldozed," said Ernie Sherman, owner of Pacific Plumbing, a former SoDo business now located in South Park, and 11 when he stared out at both capacity-filled and an empty Hooverville. "It was pretty barren after. It looked like a war zone."

Eight months before the Japanese bombed Pearl Harbor and pulled the U.S. into World War II, bulldozers roared through a vacated Hooverville and flattened the shacks, shoving them into mountainous piles before bonfires reduced everything to ashes. The transformation from homeless enclave to wartime installation, from SoDo's largest residential community on record to a steamship yard, was radical enough.

Before-and-after aerial photos tucked away as keepsakes in an office drawer of a long-time SoDo businessman, Seattle Textile owner Bill Oseran, show that half of the Hooverville land mass, so patiently and systematically created by regrade fill at the turn of the century, had disappeared in an instant with the installation of four piers

SoDo's Lady Landowner

She was an unlikely land baron, a woman with an eighth-grade education, a widow. Yet throughout the post-World War II years, Katharine "Katie" Leiendecker bought and traded properties as well as anyone in Sodo.

A short, plain woman with a bit of a temper, Leiendecker made herself noticeable with her business dealings in a male-dominated era. After her husband, Carl, died, leaving her properties purchased by her spouse and his father, she acquired several others, many along the First Avenue South corridor.

"She was an independent woman," granddaughter Margene Ridout said. "She said one of the best compliments she received was that she could think like a man."

"Real estate was like Monopoly to her," great nephew Bill Leiendecker said.

Born in Puyallup, Leiendecker had limited schooling because her father packed up the family on a scow full of cattle and moved everyone north in pursuit of Alaska Gold Rush riches. She was a self-educated woman who was very sure of herself, especially in terms of finance.

Businessmen often saw her in Seattle First National Bank arranging transactions, or arriving alone at Andy's Diner, sliding into the first table and inviting conversation.

"I'd sit with her," said Andy Yurkanin, one of two Andys who operated the restaurant. "She had a nice personality. She made a lot of money."

"She was a very, very bright gal, business-wise," seconded former SoDo business owner Art Mendelsohn.

Leiendecker lived in a modest Beacon Hill home, surrounded by items she had purchased at estate auctions, often bringing a jar of pickled herring for the auctioneer. She liked to travel, often visiting Europe and Hawaii. Otherwise, she rarely cashed in her considerable real-estate holdings. She could have used a new chair, wearing out the wooden right arm of the one she sat in for hours, stroking it methodically while bartering with bankers, realtors and others.

She had a certain amount of feistiness to her, sleeping with a .38-caliber pistol under her pillow. She wasn't afraid to use it, firing off a couple of rounds at crows invading her backyard. She wasn't trying to scare them, either.

Leiendecker was 95 when she died in 1981 at her daughter's home, not long after suffering a stroke that had her headed to an Olympia assisted-care facility, a move she really didn't want to make. Family members said she was in charge of her world to the end.

The independent Katie Leiendecker.

"She went out on her own terms," Margene Ridout said.

This woman's SoDo legacy remains firmly intact. Today, the Leiendecker Building sits at 3223 1st Avenue South, occupied by two business tenants, HealthForce and Northwest Shower Door, and is still family-owned. The Leiendecker name, in big gold letters, is affixed to the top of the two-story brick facility. A plaque, dated October 8, 1988, hangs on an outside wall near a doorway and identifies Katharine Leiendecker and other family members.

"I always asked why didn't Aunt Kate get her name on the Sears Tower?" Bill Leiendecker quipped. "She was definitely a player in that neck of the woods."

servicing naval battleships and become harbor again.

The only modern-day connection to the makeshift village was the Hooverville Bar, located at 1721 1st Avenue South, or two blocks south of where everyone once congregated in their Depression-era shacks. The drinking establishment, however, didn't have much better staying power. On February 25, 2009, after just a few years in business, the bar was gutted by fire, the cause singled out as an overheated ceiling fan. Sixty-six fire fighters were needed to put out the morning blaze, which came well after operating hours. (It later reopened that fall.)

As for the homeless, they still live in SoDo. They're just far more discreet and less organized. There is no mass gathering or waterfront village. These penniless people live wherever they can, in campers, tents and bedrolls, under viaducts and in back alleys.

The SoDo waterfront has undergone many changes over the past century-plus.

Nearly two dozen towering container cranes stand erect along the waterfront in SoDo, lined up like so many oversized robots from a Will Smith movie. They break into a rhythmic, mechanical dance whenever heavily weighted-down freighter ships sail halfway across the world, pull into the Duwamish Waterway and cast anchor.

This was Del Bates' world for 27 years. He sat in a glass cage, hovering more than 100 feet above Pier 46, receiving a turbulent ride whenever heavy wind and rain battered the city. He was a crane operator who carefully loaded and unloaded metal containers usually full of international trade but sometimes

The late Del Bates in his Seattle Angels uniform.

carrying unexpected human cargo. "I've seen stowaways, several who were Chinese," Bates said. "They opened the container and I was right there when they walked out.

> "I've seen stowaways, several who were Chinese. They opened the container and I was right there when they walked out. My thoughts were, 'Look at what they will do to get to our country.' It makes you grateful you live where you live."
>
> Del Bates

My thoughts were, 'Look at what they will do to get to our country.' It makes you grateful you live where you live."

Bates, who died in 2009,

was one of 78 crane operators spread out over three different shifts, with his preference a swing-shift slot from 3 to 8 p.m. This Port of Seattle job required three to five years of experience for someone to become readily efficient behind the intricate controls. Good hand-and-eye coordination was essential. Mistakes were expensive, if not scary. "You work with a lot of weight and you work with little tolerance," Bates explained. "I've seen several loads dropped. I've seen an excavator dropped into a hatch."

Immersed in union politics with the International Longshoreman's and Ware-

CHAPTER FIVE - PORT OF CALL

Looking to downtown Seattle from Puget Sound.

houseman's Union and its SoDo-based Local 19 when he wasn't pulling levers and enjoying one of the best views in the city, Bates maintained that his pursuit of a waterfront career was "one of the greatest decisions of my life." That's saying a lot, considering that one of his previous occupations was major league baseball player, as a catcher for the Philadelphia Phillies.

SoDo's Ever-changing Legacy

This robust, goateed man represented just a brief glimpse of SoDo's waterfront legacy that has seen this coveted property evolve over the past century from barren tideland to rickety, uneven piers to a sturdily-built World

War II military stronghold to an asphalt-covered commerce center with international connections, providing paychecks for generations to come. Seattle's earliest inhabitants attempted to claim the industrial land as their own and had to step aside when statehood and world war intervened.

This property has housed the homeless in multiple ways, not only with those inbound containers full of stowaway passengers but with the post-Depression Hooverville camp built at what is now Pier 42. To great objections, there have been modern-day proposals to make this property available to outside interests such as residential offerings, park

space, office space and even a basketball arena. But cranes and containers remain the primary tenants.

"As far as a modern city goes, we're a little unique in that we have an active,

vibrant waterfront at the foot of downtown," pointed out Charlie Sheldon, Port of Seattle's managing director of marine. "I think it's neat. You don't see other cities like that. It makes us who we

This is the first ship to transit the Panama Canal on August 15, 1914, just as World War I was erupting in Europe.

Remembering the Fallen

Jack Perry Memorial Park is a sliver of a piece of land in SoDo, invisible to all but the most observant passersby, a stark reminder that Seattle's waterfront can be a dangerous place.

The 1.1-acre park on the edge of Pier 30 at 1729 Alaskan Way South was created in 1990, two years after Perry, a 46-year-old Port of Seattle electrician, was crushed to death while performing maintenance as he worked atop a new container crane at nearby Terminal 30.

"I was in my office and I helped take him off the crane," said Jack Block Sr., then a port commissioner and someone else with a Port of Seattle park named for him in West Seattle. "He was really a nice guy. He just made a mistake getting up on top in an area he shouldn't have been in."

Jack Perry Memorial Park continues to honor a 46-year-old Port of Seattle electrician who was crushed to death while working on a new container crane at Terminal 30.

Perry, the father of three children, was 115 feet above the ground when he was killed by a piece of equipment called a sway device, which opened and closed hydraulically. He had perished before firefighters could bring him down.

In the aftermath of Perry's death, the park found at the end of a long, narrow driveway and wedged among the waterfront bustle, with 120 feet of shoreline and unobstructed views of the harbor, was christened after him.

New equipment and procedures were introduced, foremost the requirement that Port of Seattle employees work in crane safety baskets. And Perry's family was awarded $1.3 million in a wrongful death suit against the Mississippi-based crane manufacturer.

"Normally, we lose one person a year," said Block Sr., listing others who had suffered heart attacks while operating container cranes.

are."In 1905, this southern section of Seattle harbor land was home to, starting at the northern SoDo border of King Street and working its way south, the Stetson and Post Mill Company, Pacific Coast Company coal wharves, Moran Brothers Shipyard, Northern Fish Company, Centennial Milling Company, Seattle Dock Company, Hammond Milling Company and Standard Oil Company. Behind these businesses were the earliest stages of railyards rising out of the filled-in land, with plenty of marshy territory still surrounding everything to the east and south.

Modern calls to reshape SoDo into something much more diversified, to heavy industry mixed with housing and lighter industry offerings, becomes far less vocal the closer people get to the water's edge. There is no debate that Seattle has a valuable waterfront resource, and the preservation of a representative amount of blue-collar needs is necessary.

"Anywhere you have deep-draft moorage, you can't give up industrial," said Frank Firmani, a developer and former SoDo business owner. "Very few places in the world have that. We have to keep heavy industry to buffer that."

While government pursued the Seattle waterfront with controlling and economically motivated intentions beginning with statehood, nothing was permanently organized until 1911, when the Port of Seattle was created by a one-sided public vote (13,771 to 4,538). The city saw a chance to take advantage of newfound trade

"Anywhere you have deep-draft moorage, you can't give up industrial. Very few places in the world have that. We have to keep heavy industry to buffer that."

Frank Firmani

Shipbuilder Robert Moran with various U.S. Navy dignitaries on the deck of the USS Nebraska.

opportunities projected from the opening of the Panama Canal, which would be completed three years later after a decade of tedious and complicated construction across that Central American country. It was decided that people had to make well-intentioned waterfront decisions. Seattle leaders also recognized self-starter harbor development projects underway in Boston, Oakland, Philadelphia and San Francisco, and didn't want to be considered any less progressive as a seaport.

A widespread New York influence came next to help shape Seattle's waterfront. For starters, the construction of the city's piers and terminals were patterned after New York's longstanding Bush Terminals. By 1916, New York-based Todd Shipyard saw opportunity in having a business presence on each coast and purchased what was once Moran Brothers Company, Seattle's first iron and steel shipbuilding company, and the Easterners would move all operations to Harbor Island.

For that matter, the three Moran brothers, Robert, Peter and William, were native New Yorkers, with the most ambitious of the siblings, Robert, serving as Seattle mayor in 1888-1890.

The Morans were best known for building the battleship *USS Nebraska* in 1904. A reported 60,000 people showed up for an October boat launching just north of SoDo, with spectators warned in advance by Seattle newspapers to be wary that "the plunge of the *Nebraska* will raise a tidal wave." Of course, nothing happened with the ship wake to put anyone in jeopardy. The naval vessel was in service for 16 years, circling the globe and transporting World War I troops to Europe before it was decommissioned, dismantled and sold for scrap metal in 1923.

The Morans also culled considerable business from the Alaska Gold Rush, building 12 steamer ships bound for the Yukon River, with Robert Moran personally

"I would skip school on Monday afternoons and work the banana boats, which were big white boats, on Pier 5. I would line up at the longshoreman hall and pick up extra work in the summer. I worked my way through college. The old Buffalo Bag Company had a lot of stuff. Wheat went out in those burlap bags, in 150- to 160-pound bags. I can still feel it in my shoulder."

Jack Block Sr.

delivering them north.

Skinner and Eddy was another pioneering Seattle ship-builder that took advantage of significant waterfront opportunity. Located south of the Moran Brothers operation on what is now Pier 42, Skinner and Eddy built seven ships for a Norwegian customer in 1917 in less than a year, which set records for a

The SoDo waterfront was ablaze with major ship-building projects for World War II. Here's an impressive photo of the 1943 launching of the USS James E. Kyes *at Todd Shipyards.*

West Coast yard at the time. The first completed European-bound ship was outfitted in U.S. and Norway flags and festively launched in SoDo before another large gathering of waterfront spectators, though there was no journalistic hysteria warning of outlandish wake concerns for this occasion.

Port of Seattle Establishes Enduring Foothold

By the 1930s, the SoDo waterfront had much more of a Port of Seattle presence. Three large installations were mixed in among private interests. The port's Stacy Street Terminal was surrounded by open slips, the port's Lander Street terminal was pressed up against a boiler works, iron works and railroad freight dock, and the port's Hanford Street transfer shed was located next to the Isaacson Iron Works and a grain elevator. Through two world wars, the SoDo harbor proprietors experienced great boom and bust.

Overseas conflict brought nonstop nautical defense contracts and peace resulted in a noticeable shipbuilding malaise. Following World War I, Seattle's ship yards went from 20 to a handful heading into the Great Depression. During World War II, there was another upsurge in maritime business, with 46 naval destroyers constructed in these yards, which were all strictly military-controlled after Pearl Harbor was bombed.

Seattle families became waterfront staples. No one was more involved than the Blocks, who have provided three generations of dock workers and counting. This particular clan's port connection began in 1934, when George Block was bailed out of a jail stint for petty Depression-era offenses to a waiting longshoreman job. His son, Jack Block Sr., followed with 52 years of service as a longshoreman, crane operator and Port of Seattle commissioner. Grandchildren Jack

Block Jr. and Natalie Phillips collectively have served as a crane operator, computer operator and truck driver, with the former seeking and failing to land a port commissioner job.

"I would skip school on Monday afternoons and work the banana boats, which were big white boats, on Pier 5," Jack Block Sr. recalled, first unloading the imported fruit when he was 15. "I would line up at the longshoreman hall and pick up extra work in the summer. I worked my way through college. The old Buffalo Bag Company had a lot of stuff. Wheat went out in those burlap bags, in 150- to 160-pound bags. I can still feel it in my shoulder."

Post-WWII Waterfront Expansion

Once World War II fighting was done, SoDo's waterfront expansion began in earnest. Piers were reclaimed. Piers were rebuilt. Money was pumped into the Duwamish

Massive ships and the containers they carry began revolutionizing the character of SoDo in the mid-1960s.

Waterway development. Railroad Avenue, providing direct access to the water's edge for incoming and outgoing cargo, was widened, paved and renamed Alaskan Way after brief consideration was given to calling it Sea-Port Way. In 1953, this roadway was given yet another name, East Marginal Way, when an overhead viaduct was installed and identified as Alaskan Way. Increased post-war auto traffic made it difficult to move truck shipments to and from the waterfront, necessitating the viaduct.

Establishing the Industrial Zone & Containerizing

At the time, a city planning commission report decided that all land west of the new viaduct was to have industrial use only; all property east of it would be considered for commercial or major business. More than five decades later, that badly needed Alaskan Way Viaduct had become obsolete and an earthquake hazard, and was headed for a wrecking ball and waterfront tunnel replacement. The Port of Seattle's first profit, $88,000, was reported in 1954.

There was great build-up and momentum to an innovation only a few saw coming: Containerization.

"My dad was pretty forward-thinking and he said the container would be the answer, that it would be wall to wall," Jack Block Sr. said. "He worked for Mattson and they were the first ones to have container ships, the first to put containers on deck."

Containers, virtually large, reusable metal boxes, introduced dramatic change to ocean shipping. Cargo could now be unloaded in a day whereas it previously required

A Union Neighborhood

Organized labor couldn't be any better organized than it is in the SoDo District, at least geographically. A union hall sits on every major thoroughfare that cuts north and south through the working man's neighborhood.

From the waterfront moving inland, the International Organization of Masters Mates (pilots) is headquartered at 1727 Alaskan Way South, the International Longshoremen's and Warehousemen's Union Local 19 at 3440 East Marginal Way South, the United Food and Commercial Workers Union at 5030 1st Avenue South, the Seattle Education Association at 5501 4th Avenue South, the Seattle Police Guild at 2949 4th Avenue South, the Bakery and Confectionary Workers Union at 5950 6th Avenue South, and the Service Employees International Union at 3720 Airport Way South.

"In terms of an industrial base, that's the core of Seattle," said David Freiboth, King County Labor Council executive secretary, referring to SoDo.

Labor and union protection has gone hand in hand practically since the first shovel of fill was tossed on the former tideland. A makeshift longshoreman's union actually appeared in Seattle almost a full decade before the industrial area started to take shape. SoDo shared in the tension and violence wrought by the 1934 waterfront strike that would shut down all West Coast shipping operations with an 83-day walkout. Trains were blocked by idle workers. Police and picketers engaged in shoving matches. Two people, a strike leader and a sheriff's deputy, were killed during the animosities.

Jack Block Sr., son of a Seattle longshoreman, was born near the end of that strike. He would follow his father onto the waterfront and at 28 become one of the youngest union delegates elected, at

International Organization of Masters Mates

International Longshoremen's and Warehousemen's Union Local 19

United Food and Commercial Workers Union

Seattle Education Association

Seattle Police Guild

Bakery and Confectionary Workers Union

Service Employees International Union

31 become the coast's youngest foreman and later pull several terms as a port commissioner.

"When you got out of high school, you went to jail, the military or, if your dad was a longshoreman, you went down there and worked as a casual (or part-timer)," Block said. "If your dad was a longshoreman and he got hurt, you would get his book and be expected to take care of the family. You would get put on the 'B' list and move right into the 'A' list, kind of like coal miners, and we had that tradition since 1934."

Not long after that, Dave Beck came to power as a Seattle labor leader, using his considerable influence to assume control of the national labor movement as president of the International Brotherhood of the Teamsters. Typical of his efforts, Beck encouraged a newspaper strike by enlisting waterfront workers to show up and form rowdy picket lines for the more white-collar personnel.

Another sample of the influence labor wields came when all Seattle port operations were shut down for an hour in 1996 after deceased longshoreman labor leader Martin Jugum was eulogized in a Harbor Island warehouse and his ashes were spread just off SoDo in the Duwamish Waterway by family members.

Freiboth, the county labor leader, was a ferry worker for a dozen years who joined union activities in a logical if not impatient manner. "I got of sick of people complaining about the union, so I got involved in politics," he said. Freiboth has made it one of his chief labor goals to prevent SoDo from giving up any of its industrial influence in favor of commercial and residential offerings.

"It's going to take an effort," he said. "It's something I'm very

(continued on page 56)

four to five monotonous days. Goods were locked tight and better protected against ever-present pier theft. In 1964, the Port of Seattle opened its first container facility at Pier 46, setting up two 45-ton cranes on 21 acres of dock and open storage space at a cost of $8 million. That same year, the port also purchased four former army piers (36-39), accompanying buildings and 22 acres for $4 million, intended to support a super-terminal for containers. The investment was an insightful one, particularly when coupled with a new freeway nearby running north and south.

"In 1965, Interstate 5 was built and the big leap came next to the container world," pointed out Tom McQuaid, owner of SoDo's Nordic Cold Storage. "You didn't see tractor-trailers anymore. You saw containers taking goods to market or recycling. You saw little rail traffic going into the waterfront; very little rail. It was all containers. There was no need for the railyard.

The container revolutionized everything."

Seattle's Port Climbs in the World Rankings

As a result, the Puget Sound region experienced a nautical rush hour. There was no better evidence of this than in late December in 1966, when a record 47 ships sailed into the inland waters in a single day, with another nine ships already idle for repair or other reasons, sending the Seattle waterfront support systems into an absolute mad scramble. Tugboat pilots and customs' and agriculture inspectors could hardly keep up with the increased work load. Longshoreman crews were shuttled from pier to pier to unload waiting cargo, but there was still a shortage of available manpower.

Over the next decade, Port of Seattle foreign trade expanded by 111 percent. Jobs increased from 16,000 to 25,000. Cargo tonnage handled went from 2.2 million

to 6.5 million. From a handful of Port of Seattle facilities in use, nearly the entire SoDo waterfront was paved over, dressed up with container cranes and turned into something shipping-related. Outdated facilities such as grain elevators, coal-loading operations and various warehouses were removed and military holdings were reclaimed.

"In 1965, Interstate 5 was built and the big leap came next to the container world. You didn't see tractor-trailers anymore. You saw containers taking goods to market or recycling. You saw little rail traffic going into the waterfront; very little rail. It was all containers. There was no need for the railyard. The container revolutionized everything."

Tom McQuaid

Amid this waterfront frenzy of activity, imported goods to Seattle's waterfront at one point were broken down this way: 80 percent came from Transpacific ports, seven percent from Europe, seven percent from Hawaii and six percent from Alaska. Similarly, Seattle exports were sent out in the following manner: 56 percent to Alaska, 27 percent to Trans-pacific ports, 10 percent to Europe and Latin America and seven percent to Hawaii. The current SoDo waterfront lineup, from north to south, offers a sprawling Port of Seattle container yard, Coast Guard facilities and cutter moorage, a Federal warehouse, Pacific Maritime Technical and Career Center that serves as a training center and pilots' union hall, the Jack Perry Memorial Park, and another sizeable Port of Seattle container yard that bumps up against the West Seattle Freeway.

(continued from page 54)
vigilant about. It's going to take some stewardship that it's always going to be there. Some would charge that it's been eroded away. I don't feel that it's at a tipping point, but we have to defend and husband what we have. Overall, the job creation here is pretty much still the engine of Seattle."

While SoDo remains a natural haven for the common union worker, with its industry-based jobs seemingly well-protected and politicians bent on keeping them that way, the area proved to be a place of great comfort, from an entertainment standpoint, for the city's most notorious labor boss in his waning years. Dave Beck, who was 99 when he died in 1993, spent most summer nights at the Kingdome, watching his beloved Mariners play. He no doubt would be satisfied with the way union-influenced SoDo has turned out in his absence.

"I think he would be happy with how Seattle has grown up and maintained its uniqueness and diversity, though he wouldn't use the word diversity, which came after his time," Freiboth said.

Harbor Island

SoDo also claims as its own nearby Harbor Island, another section of former tideland full of ship ballast and turned into pilings and fill and blacktop. It's no different than having a moon orbiting the main planet. Container yards take up most of the satellite property, with Shell and Arco oil facilities wedged into the middle of the shipping activity. What's left of the now-named Todd Pacific Shipyards occupies only the northwestern corner of the island, whereas once it filled up three of the four corners. Ten blue shipyard cranes mostly sit idle above well-worn structures lining this part of the harbor. The Todd Pacific workforce has been pared from a high of 7,000 to maybe 500 in 2009. There is more ship repair than ship-building done there now, though Todd Pacific continues to bid on new ferry work. From Harbor Island to Pier 46 at the northern tip of SoDo, the Port of Seattle's container crane population stands at 23, with 18 of them painted orange, four coming in white and one a shade of blue.

SoDo's Waterfront Evolution – Here to Stay?

In modern times, the SoDo waterfront has gone from wildly expansionist times fueled by the Alaska Gold Rush and container-yard evolution to a more sedate protectionist period of maintaining the shipping offerings while entertaining and dismissing creative ideas to wrest its property away.

A 1998 city strategic planning office study geared for the waterfront neighborhood promised to come up with a plan that allowed "the Duwamish to grow with grace." To that end, city planners suggested land-use controls and transportation system improvements were the only alternatives.

The study concluded that "ocean shipping, tug and barge operations, and ship and boat building do not have the option to relocate to Kent Valley." Mayor Greg Nickels seconded these SoDo findings when he proclaimed, "Seattle's industrial lands are a finite resource. Once they are taken out of industrial use, it would be difficult, if not impossible, to create more industrial land. There is continuing high industrial demand for the limited land zoned industrial today."

Sheldon, the port's maritime leader, seconded that idea: "There is a lot of gentrification taking place, bit by bit. But there is also a lot of maintenance (of work space) going on. By and large, I think a lot of people like this working waterfront nature of this city."

The study concluded that "ocean shipping, tug and barge operations, and ship and boat building do not have the option to relocate to Kent Valley."

Seattle city councilman Bruce Harrell offered this cautious vision: "We are a port city. It would be nice to keep the character conducive to that type of industrial area. That's not saying there aren't areas available for retail use, but I don't see a wholesale overhaul of that crane area."

Far-Reaching Attempt Doesn't Get too Far

That hasn't stopped others from trying to create significant SoDo change, especially involving the hands-off waterfront holdings. In 2003, SoDo developers Greg Smith and Frank Stagen, in concert with Seahawks' owner and Microsoft co-founder Paul Allen, drew up and presented an ambitious plan to turn Pier 46 into a modern waterfront community. They proposed building 4,000 apartments and condominiums, combining them with office and research space, and tying everything together with an elaborate

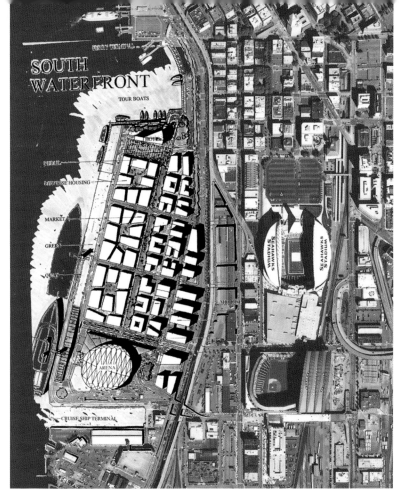

The concept phase of an ambitious plan by SoDo developers Greg Smith and Frank Stagen, along with Seahawks' owner and Microsoft co-founder Paul Allen.

park area that had an artificial lake and an Elliott Bay lock. There were suggestions of putting a pro basketball arena into this mix, something that would lure the NBA back to Seattle (though the Sonics were still playing at Key Arena at the time of the study). There also were provisions for bringing Seattle ferry traffic from the central waterfront through SoDo's Pier 37, over an elevated South Royal

Brougham Way and funneling it directly to Interstates 5 and 90.

With future Alaskan Way Viaduct replacement anticipated, these developers saw a chance to offer something different to the city, if not an opportunity to "green up" an asphalt-covered area full of metal containers that might not be as busy as before. Their residential mock-up was hailed by some city leaders as innovative and well worth exploring. They saw it as a way to dress up SoDo's slow-to-develop stadium district, by starting on the waterfront and moving inland.

Port of Seattle – and Others – Resistant to Change

However, the Port of Seattle, citing long-term contracts and options with foreign shipping companies, specifically Japan's Hanjiin, ultimately dismissed the idea. Pier 46 likely represents the last piece of waterfront

Eisenhower in SoDo

Presidential motorcades have crisscrossed SoDo on more than one occasion. Barack Obama made multiple campaign visits to Seattle's industrial district. George Bush Sr. and Bill Clinton have been among the nation's top leaders who were whisked through the area en route to a waiting Air Force One jet at nearby Boeing Field.

In 1952, Gen. Dwight Eisenhower, a World War II hero bidding to become the nation's 34ᵗʰ President, drove up the middle of SoDo in a scene forever lost in another, more innocent time. Escorted by a couple of Seattle motorcycle police officers and little more, Ike sat in an open-air car as it wove through the southern part of town.

There was almost no one on the streets to greet the candidate, with the exception of Doug Glant, 9, and his grandfather Jules Glant. They stood together on the steps of the family-owned Pacific Iron and Metal Company at 2230 4ᵗʰ Avenue South, anticipating Eisenhower's arrival in the neighborhood.

"My grandfather whistled at him, and said, 'Wave, Dougy!' and I waved," recounted Doug Glant, now a co-owner of Pacific Iron and Metal. "Eisenhower saw me and waved back and he was on his way down the street. That's my favorite memory."

In 1952, Gen. Dwight Eisenhower, a World War II hero bidding to become the nation's 34th President, came through SoDo with a minimum of fanfare. Here is what would become the 34th President of the United States in his five-star general's uniform.

property the port would be willing to deal. Built on double pilings, this facility sits next to water that runs 80 feet deep, deeper than anywhere else at the harbor's edge. "They've got enough condos in Seattle," Block Sr. said. "You can put them on the hills. They don't need this."

While this particular gentrification idea didn't materialize, there are people who still insist this type of land conversion is inevitable for SoDo and the rest of Seattle, particularly in places hugging the waterfront. Doug Rosen, Alaskan Copper Works vice president and a real-estate developer, is a proponent of this forward thinking. He points to Portland's Pearl District as the perfect example of mixing residential and industrial together. "It was forever industrial property," he said of the old Pearl District. "It was old railyards and old industrial buildings. That was 10 years ago. They've turned

it into an incredible area. The same is true of Portland's south waterfront. They have cable cars coming down the hill, bio-tech, research labs and high-rise condos. Seattle has changed a little but it's very slow."

The developers behind the Pier 46 project heard objections from Seattle's professional sports teams occupying Safeco Field and Qwest Field, with those tenants fearful that waterfront residential offerings would block their fans' harbor views. There also were concerns that the added traffic would back up outbound trucks hauling containers, and the nearby Seattle International Gateway (SIG) railyard south of the pier in question would become underutilized.

Between the port and the pro teams, that was enough opposition to put the elaborate proposal on a back burner. Yet the masterminds behind the waterfront conversion haven't given up. They'll wait for the right fiscal time to promote another project, seeking a more receptive audience.

"When you're looking long term for the ports of Seattle and Tacoma and economic development, you have to get the shipping containers in," Greg Smith conceded. "But as technology improves and containers can be moved through less land, are there opportunities for the Port of Seattle to deal with the container industry and create bright, intelligent development for the community? We thought Pier 46 was one of those opportunities."

Certain American manufacturing interests steadily have been outsourced to Asian markets. Yet port authorities suggest that increasing transportation fuel costs and shortages ultimately could negate the labor savings that prompted this radical shift, possibly requiring a return of industry to its U.S. origins, which would include SoDo. Any more container yard expansion is unlikely, but it's important to maintain what's in place.

Give up the land now, the argument is repeated over and over, and it won't be reclaimed later. "There may be more cargo, though it won't be as great or expanding as fast as before," the port's Sheldon pointed out.

For now, those towering robots that double as container cranes remain firmly in place, protectors of heavy industry – SoDo sentries stubbornly resistant to change on the waterfront.

Chapter Six

There Goes the Neighborhood

The break-up was a tough one. Puget Sound Pipe and Supply Company had conducted business in the SoDo District for nearly eight decades and the connection was over. Founded by Austrian immigrant Ire Stratiner, who was sent to Alaska by an outfit that sold toilets and stopped in Seattle and liked it so much he traveled no farther, his was a pipe-peddling firm created in 1917 that was big on family. It was a business that Stratiner eventually turned over to his son, Phillip, who in turn handed it over to his son, Gary.

"He started in a building at First and Horton," Gary Stratiner said of his grandfather. "He was always working outside with a couple of goats who were eating the grass."

Puget Sound Pipe and Supply Company founder Ire Stratiner with two of his goats in front of his business.

Some Originals Start Looking Elsewhere

Yet by 1994, this long-term relationship between the Stratiners and SoDo, like so many tired marriages, had become strained and no longer tolerable. Puget Sound Pipe and Supply moved out.

This was part of a mass exodus out of SoDo by several businesses bound for the suburbs south of Seattle, namely Renton, Kent and Auburn. This was a movement fueled by seemingly unlimited warehouse space and often offered at one-third the price. This concentrated shift in work-place addresses began in earnest in the early 1980s and currently remains in play, with

longtime Seattle originals such as Star Machinery, Howard-Cooper Corporation, Western Marine, Alaska Distributors, Music-Vend and Golden Grain among the weighty companies that fled the big city for outlying areas. Alaskan Copper, the biggest one yet to leave, soon will complete the transfer of its warehouse business – which operates under the name of Alaskan Copper and Brass – to a Kent site while keeping its manufacturing and head offices intact on 6th Avenue South in SoDo.

"It was a SoDo sell-off and relocation, coming during the Reagan Depression," explained Art Mendelsohn, a SoDo businessman for 57 years until his retirement, and someone who avoided this calamity by finding a buyer for his equipment yard. "It was healthy. Only the strongest remained."

Not necessarily. Some of the strongest moved away, too. The Stratiners bought a 12-acre property in Kent, one of the last available industrial pieces in the northern portion of that south King County city. It was either take that site or move to Auburn, or go even farther south. The family set up business on a quiet road that led to railway tracks and had no regrets whatsoever. They said goodbye to SoDo and easily moved on.

"The best thing we ever did was come down here," Gary Stratiner said. "It was just a question of when, not if, if we wanted to continue growth."

Increasing Compression Leads to Migration

In SoDo, Puget Sound Pipe and Supply had dealt with a glaring problem that wouldn't go away: its trucks and business orders had gotten a lot bigger while Seattle's industrial space seemed to be shrinking, and the squeeze was costing the Stratiners a great deal of money. Every last bit of SoDo property was occupied by someone, leaving no room for expansion.

Because of rising demand this grimy yet centralized real estate had become far more valuable, with higher taxes cutting into profits. Add to that deliveries and pick-ups that were near impossible to make, and a move became inevitable.

Puget Sound Pipe and Supply's business was flourishing, but there was not enough storage space at 3223 3rd Avenue South, property that the family had owned since 1968. Arrangements were made for a short-term solution that didn't last long. Pipe was stacked in a nearby Andy's Diner parking lot, on railroad-owned land, yet when that lease expired the diner was given exclusive rights to the

"It was a SoDo sell-off and relocation, coming during the Reagan Depression. It was healthy. Only the strongest remained."

Art Mendelsohn

lease and the coveted space.

Trucks coming into the area were longer now – negotiating SoDo streets with 53 feet of trailer length, whereas the traditional 48-footers already had enough trouble maneuvering around the area. Traffic, likewise, had worsened, with car volumes way up as retail space brought in more workers and customers. Street parking has always been a nightmare. Something had to give for Puget Sound Pipe and Supply, and the suburbs were the answer.

"Come in on Mondays and we have six trucks loaded up with pipe and they get unloaded in an hour, where it would have taken us a week before," Stratiner said of his advantageous Kent headquarters for the past 15 years.

Puget Sound Pipe and Supply moved into 79,000 square feet of warehouse and office space, nearly double what it had in SoDo. There was far greater freedom to fill orders now. Supplying Alaskan customers with pipe, valves and

"Come in on Mondays and we have six trucks loaded up with pipe and they get unloaded in an hour, where it would have taken us a week before."

Gary Stratiner

fittings represents 60 percent of the business and demands greater space. Customers up north have included British Petroleum, Coneco Phillips and Alyeska refinery operations. Previously, the biggest pipe buyers were local shipyards Todd, Lockheed and Tacoma, before they all downsized or went out of business. There are 50 Puget Sound Pipe and Supply employees now, twice the manpower the company once had. Everything became bigger and better.

"We have three and a half to four acres of paved, lit-up power yard to move pipe around," Stratiner said. "We put in a couple of aircraft doors and we can bring

SoDo & the Race to Space

A neighborhood that once had trouble keeping its head above water now has its head in the clouds. The Space Shuttle doesn't leave the ground without help from SoDo.

Since 1993, two gigantic cranes built at the former Ederer plant at 2937 South Utah Street have been used to prepare various shuttle missions in the Vertical Assembly Building of the Kennedy Space Center outside Orlando, Fla. The Ederer cranes were requisitioned following the Challenger shuttle tragedy in 1986. NASA decided it needed bigger and better equipment as replacements for cranes previously brought in during the mid-1960s for use with the Apollo program.

"We still point to it as the hallmark project for the company," said Neil Skogland, crane segment manager for Ederer, which has Seattle home offices yet moved its manufacturing plant to Georgia. "It's still one of the most sophisticated cranes in the world."

Built over two years and delivered by several truck caravans traveling between Seattle and the Florida coast, these space-age cranes have girders pieced together in four segments, each measuring 70 feet long and weighing around 70 tons each. Similar to the retractable Safeco Field roof built by Ederer, the cranes came equipped with wheels that travel by rail along the top.

The hard part was adapting the cranes to a Vertical Assembly Building that stands nearly as tall as Seattle's 605-foot Space Needle. The advantage was in having cranes so powerful and intricate in operation that assurances could be given that another Challenger tragedy and O-ring failure would not be repeated.

"They said we have to replace these cranes because we don't have the kind of control we thought we had or need," former Ederer Crane owner Don Miller explained. "The critical part of the new crane was control. When we completed this crane, we had done something literally never done before."

One of Ederer Crane's most famous projects was the two gigantic cranes that have been used to prepare various shuttle missions at Kennedy Space Center.

44-foot pieces of pipe in sideways. Before, with a crane, it was very cumbersome."

Losing Long-Term Local Customers but Broadening Markets

The downside to moving out was losing long-term Seattle customers because Kent wasn't convenient for them. But Puget Sound Pipe and Supply's ability to move more of its products at a rapidly accelerated rate more than offset the losses.

"It was a lot of history and we walked away from some key accounts that we had in that area," Stratiner said. "We knew they wouldn't be buying as much because we knew they couldn't come down and pick it up. But we did a demographic where the supplies were going, and we were determined to pick up as much, if not more, by coming down south. We've seen a lot of people in our industry move down here in

The Alaskan Copper & Brass Company logo outside their offices.

the valley. Doing business in Seattle isn't the easiest.

"It's the same kind of problem California has. They chased everybody out and they went other places."

Holding Down Two Forts

Alaskan Copper owns more SoDo property than anyone except the Port of Seattle and real estate developer Henry Liebman, yet it doesn't have enough to keep all of its business holdings operating effectively inside the city.

"We have more than half of our wholesale business in Renton, and we've been shipping between two areas," explained Alaskan Copper & Brass vice president Doug Rosen, one of four brothers and a cousin who run the

family-owned company. "We're consolidating our warehouse. We've been very inefficient."

To facilitate the move in stages, the Rosens leased property in Renton while purchasing and preparing an old aluminum can plant in Kent for consolidation of all its warehouse business. Once everything is in place, Alaskan Copper and Brass will have 120,000 square feet of work space in hand.

> "Of 100 customers, 80 of them were within a mile of our shop. If we were there now, only two companies would do business with us that close."
>
> Dave Ederer

"These businesses are no longer functional in the city," Alaskan Copper president Bill Rosen said. "We need cheap land, noisy and dirty."

Straying Even Further Afield

Ederer Crane was a SoDo presence for nine decades, but overseas crane building done with deeply discounted rates cut into the business and splintered operations. No longer family-run, the company keeps its corporate headquarters in Seattle but has moved its manufacturing to a Georgia plant because that's even cheaper than Kent.

"Of 100 customers, 80 of them were within a mile of our shop," Dave Ederer said.

SoDo & the World Trade Center

SoDo can't have high-rise buildings. Seattle zoning restrictions have kept it mostly at warehouse height, mixed with a couple of stadiums, some mid-rise structures allowed on the northern fringe of the area and, of course, the exception to the neighborhood rule, the Sears Building turned SoDo Center turned Starbucks Center.

Yet when terrorists flew a pair of Boeing 767 jets into the World Trade Center's "Twin Towers" in Lower Manhattan and sent the buildings crashing to the ground in 2001, part of SoDo came down with them.

Of the 230,000 tons of structural steel used to erect the 110-story buildings, 55,000 tons were supplied by Seattle's Pacific Car and Foundry Company (PACCAR), which was located at 80 South Hudson Street on the southern edge of SoDo.

Jim White, now president of Seattle-based Mobile Crane, a company formerly named Western Bridge and founded by his father, reveals this now. When the World Trade Center's North and South towers were completed in 1970 and 1971, respectively, White was an East Coast resident working on the massive project.

"I had some involvement in the World Trade Center," he said coyly, not wishing to offer many concrete details about himself.

White said the steel used in the construction of the New York towers was acquired from fabricators in Pittsburgh, St. Louis, Los Angeles, Houston and Seattle, the latter specifically identified as SoDo's PACCAR, a multi-faceted company mostly known for truck production but also into other fabricating ventures through the 1970s.

"There was a large charge of steel in the debris field, three columns of plates crossing through, and you could see it coming down from an angle, and that stuff came from Pacific Car and Foundry," White said.

55,000 tons of the structual steel used to erect The World Trade Center Towers were supplied by Seattle's Pacific Car and Foundry Company (PACCAR)

"If we were there now, only two companies would do business with us that close."

Alaska Distributors is one of the more recent departures, moving to Kent in 2006 after spending 44 years in SoDo. A third-generation company owned by the Loeb family until recent consolidation with four other companies, this beer and soft drink supplier couldn't get the job done with 277,000 square feet of work space at 4601 6th Avenue South. It has an enormous 450,000 square feet at its disposal in the suburbs now.

Logistical stuff, more than anything, was the problem. The space adjoining Alaska Distributors was railroad-owned land that was leased out to other concerns, preventing access to one side of the freight terminal. This was hardly ideal for a company receiving 25 trailer loads of beverages and sending out 60 to 70 trucks daily.

"We only had 29 doors to get in and out; the building we moved into has 92 doors," said Steve Loeb, Alaska Distributors president and chief executive officer. "A distributor wants to receive on one side and ship out on the other, and we were going in and out of the same doors. It was really inefficient. We had inadequate parking for trailers. They were sitting in the middle of 6th Avenue, or sitting in Tukwila, waiting for an appointment to deliver."

Price is Right in the Suburbs

It's not hard to see the business attraction to Kent and its surrounding areas now put to serious industrial strength use, for one reason alone: The price is right. Consider that SoDo land sells for $45 to $75 per square foot; in Kent, it goes for $9 to $15 per square foot. SoDo warehouse space leases for 60 cents per square foot; in Kent, it can be had for 34 to 36 cents per square foot. And concentrated SoDo car and truck-parking

"If you want to see what Seattle used to be like, go to Monterrey, Mexico. There are 100 business parks, all hardcore machinery. We go down there and see all of the work we used to do 30 years ago."

Dave Ederer

space leases for 20 cents per square foot; south of Auburn, it's practically a giveaway at seven cents a square foot.

"That's a big savings," said Gary Volchok, a C.B. Richard Ellis real-estate agent who brokered the Puget Sound Pipe and Supply move south. "You've got millions of square feet in the valley compared to what's in SoDo. The problem presently is the price of land is so high in SoDo new industry can't afford to come in and buy land or build a building, or buy and build."

In SoDo, a new tenant with big space needs likely has to set up shop in a

70-year-old building that could use an upgrade or two. In south King County, the warehouses usually are no older than two decades, still modern in appearance.

Kent typically offers warehouses of up to 80,000 to 100,000 square feet. Significant space in SoDo is usually no more than 30,000 square feet.

"Woody walk-ups don't rent well," said Frank Firmani, Seattle contractor and real estate developer, chiding the older SoDo buildings.

It's clear the dynamics of doing business in SoDo have changed dramatically. Where the neighborhood once was the poor stepchild of Seattle, it now rates as a blood relative. This has caused the warehouse move to the suburbs, coming on the heels of most manufacturing shops leaving the area altogether – or completely disappearing.

The original Star Machinery eventually shifted its business focus to equipment rentals due to heightened competition from Japanese manufacturers who offered cheaper equipment.

Change Happens Quickly in the Business World

Star Machinery once was the flagship business for the Rabel family, together with Star Rentals forming SoDo's longest continuously running business (109 years). The machine division moved into a newly built, state-of-the-art plant erected in the middle of the industrial district, opening to rave reviews in 1953. Within a few decades, it had become obsolete. Star Machinery next moved into another newly built, though smaller, building in Renton in an effort to save the floundering business, but it was too late. By the late 1980s, the assets of the manufacturing shop gradually were sold off and the remaining business was pared down and ultimately handed over to a manager to run by himself.

"We were getting eaten alive by little storefronts that only sold machinery, had no services shop and had two people in the field for every one person in the office," Star Rentals co-owner Bill Rabel said. "We were geared for full service, with a service shop and parts department, lots of clerical, and two people inside for every one outside. We whittled it down to try and compete with the little storefronts."

If that wasn't competition enough, Star Machinery also was up against Japanese manufacturers who entered the marketplace with far cheaper equipment, leading the Rabels to finally take drastic action and concentrate solely on their expanding rentals division.

Big industrial shops not only have deserted SoDo over the past two decades, some of them didn't stop moving until they had crossed well over the U.S.-Mexican border.

"If you want to see what Seattle used to be like, go to Monterrey, Mexico," Dave Ederer pointed out. "There are 100 business parks, all hardcore machinery. We go down there and see all of the work we used to do 30 years ago."

Holding on for the Long Haul

The suburbs have been good for business, even allowing one prominent company to go full circle in terms of location. While maintaining its Kent warehouse, Puget Sound Pipe and Supply actually returned to SoDo, in a pared-down version, leasing a 10,000-square-foot facility from the McKinstry Company in order to satisfy the needs of its smaller group of local and loyal customers.

As for being forced to abandon their main SoDo plants and take their businesses south, the Stratiners and the other family-owned businesses don't want or need anyone's sympathy. They might have moved or are moving their equipment and employees, but memories and sentiment are all that's being sacrificed. These families might have changed work addresses or are in the process of changing them at considerable expense, but

they aren't giving up the SoDo properties that will be vacated. They're holding on tight. The only loser here likely is the city and its tax base.

SoDo might not fit current business models, but the place still looks good on a portfolio. The Stratiners, Loebs and Rosens will hang on to their properties, maybe lease them, maybe not. They'll no doubt profit handsomely some day, but not just now. SoDo land is far too valuable to part with at this juncture, and it's only going to increase.

"That's one reason I'm very reluctant to sell the property we have down there," Gary Stratiner allowed. "My father said everything is going to move in that direction some day and be worth more money. It's probably gone up 10 times since we left."

CHAPTER SIX - THERE GOES THE NEIGHBORHOOD

Chapter Seven

Name That Tideflat

Welcome
TO
SODO
BUSINESS
DISTRICT
5050 BLDG.

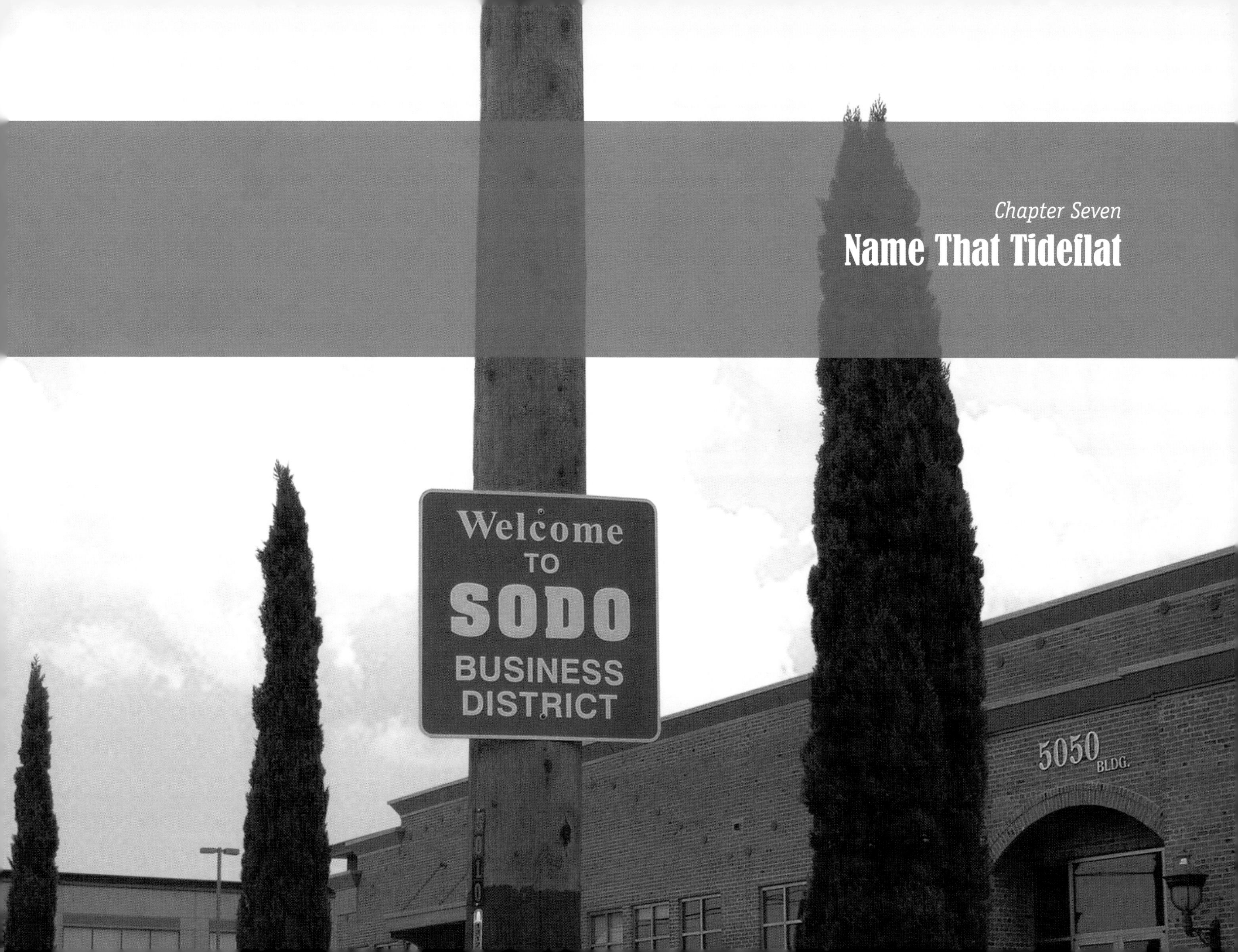

SoDo was no different than the scraggly and cranky feral cat that now resides in the back of the well-worn Amick Metal Fabricators building on Sixth Avenue South, or the equally anonymous rats that scamper through the back alleys of the neighborhood. It didn't have a name.

For more than eight decades, this had been a productive yet colorless community, operating without proper identification. It had been transformed from tideflat to dirt to asphalt without having a christening. And while other corners of the city were assigned the regal labels

Peter Miller is the one who originally called the industrial area on Seattle's south side SoDo.

of Queen Anne, Beacon Hill and Capitol Hill, this part of town always signed in with an "X" and answered only to "Hey you!"

Politicians long referred to

this place in their technically correct policy statements and file documents as "the Duwamish Manufacturing and Industrial Center," or "the North Duwamish Industrial Area," or "South Seattle Industrial Park," or even "Greater Duwamish," identifiers that didn't show up anywhere on city maps or reflect the colonizing efforts of some respected and long since-departed pioneer.

It took Peter Miller, a transplanted New Englander and then an eager journalist for the Seattle Weekly, to act as next of kin and provide the area an ID. It took a 1979 trip to New York City, not his native New Haven, Conn., for Miller to come up with his needed inspiration. It took one look

Miller should have been taking bows, blowing kisses and signing autographs. Instead, he was treated like the comedian who threw out his best punch line, heard uncomfortable silence and then back-pedaled off the stage.

at a newly reinvented part of industrialized Gotham named Soho (for south of Houston Street, and borrowed from London's historic district) while attending a book show for this man to come back to the Northwest, take another glance at Seattle and its blocks of warehouses and machine shops, and propose a similar moniker – SoDo, for south of the Dome. It meant south of the Kingdome. It meant something to Miller, but it meant absolutely nothing to anyone else.

For such devoted civic responsibility, Miller should have been taking bows, blowing kisses and signing autographs. Instead, he was treated like the comedian who threw out his best punch line, heard uncomfortable silence and then backpedaled off the stage.

"I can promise you no one cared," Miller recalled. "They really didn't care. There was no reason to. There was nothing going on down there. They didn't even care about SoDo."

He had shared all of this brainstorming with Seattle Weekly publisher David Brewster. Miller told Brewster he would write annual stories about his new creation and all its trappings, but received a similarly disinterested response from his boss and let it go.

"I said, 'We should call it SoDo,' where you can get a vacuum cleaner repaired and where you can go get something to eat," said Miller, now an uptown architectural-book peddler and casual Seattle Weekly contributor. "But in those days, there was only

One of the original SoDo signs still intact is on the side of this parking garage next to Seattle's new light-rail train station.

Andy's Diner down there. I said SoDo, and Brewster chuckled. I didn't think it would ever come up again."

Lo & Behold, Look What Reappears

Ten years would pass before a form of spontaneous combustion took place at the Seattle Weekly offices, with SoDo arbitrarily pulled out of a

bottom drawer. A senior editor, Rose Pike, and a project writer, Eric Scigliano, people with East Coast and Midwest backgrounds, respectively, would collaborate on a feature story about this forgotten neighborhood now showing signs of coming to life. They needed a hook, something to draw readers to their work. They sat in their downtown office and tossed ideas back and forth like two people playing fairly serious tennis, lobbing shots at each other.

They tried out SoRo or SoBro, both for South of Royal Brougham Way, a street named after a huckster journalist, the Seattle Post-Intelligencer's dearly departed sports editor and self-styled civic promoter. They attempted to lump it with SoSpo, for the section south of Spokane Street. To encompass everything, they settled on something the alternative newspaper had considered before: SoDo.

"We were batting it around, and I can't remember who

This picture was taken at the Starbucks re-dedication September 20, 2002. From left to right: Peter Nitze, Placido Arango Jr., Kevin Daniels, Frank Stagen, Orin Smith and Steve DuBrul. Peter, Kevin, Frank and Steve served as the general partners for the project, while Placido Jr. was a major investor from Spain. Orin Smith was President and CEO of Starbucks at the time.

to remodel it and reinvigorate it. That meant fresh paint. That meant new space. That meant eventually removing the old name from atop this beacon of business and slapping on a new one. In this case, the new one was an old one.

"I thought the SoDo name was interesting and put it on the list for Frank's consideration," said Daniels, who had filed away the aforementioned Seattle Weekly article for future reference.

Stagen had to come up with a name of five letters or fewer in order to satisfy the building code in place. He considered the options. He

thought of that one," said Scigliano, now an editor for Seattle Metropolitan magazine. "It was Rose Pike who came up with the idea for the story. I wrote it. We brainstormed together. SoDo was the name we came up with. It was, 'Oh, sure, like Soho in London's red light district.'"

In 1991, now more than a decade following Miller's divine inspiration, transplanted New York developers Frank Stagen and Kevin Daniels of Nitze-Stagen engineered the acquisition of the vacated Sears Building. Their plan was

"Everybody fought real hard against the name – the community, the real estate community. They thought it was a silly name. Everybody did. They said it doesn't mean anything."

Frank Stagen

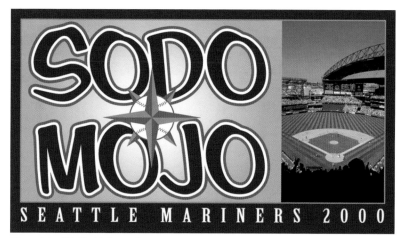

The original SoDo Mojo poster.

picked SoDo. He didn't satisfy everyone. Check that, he didn't satisfy anyone.

"Everybody fought real hard against the name – the community, the real estate community," Stagen said. "They thought it was a silly name. Everybody did. They said it doesn't mean anything. It sounds Asian. They said it sounded Japanese. Racism? That's why I'm not mentioning any business names now. It was catchy and we could put up four big letters. It was no more complicated than that."

At the time, resourceful and aggressive Japanese businessmen were buying up precious American real estate throughout the country at an alarming rate to some, acquiring properties such as Pebble Beach Golf Resort that effectively created an instant racist backlash in this country. Stagen ignored the Seattle protests, unconcerned about any cultural misinterpretation and settled on a name. He had four signs of four red block letters fastened to each side of the building tower, advertising SoDo in every direction.

Yet it wasn't nearly enough for unanimous acceptance throughout the city. Most outsiders still referred to this neglected neighborhood that held the Kingdome and the newly refurbished and renamed Sears Building and surrounding businesses as nothing more than the "Industrial Area." Generic still stumped the brand name that wouldn't go away.

"It was South of the Dome, but the Dome was the only thing, and the poor Dome nearly wiped out all of Pioneer Square," Miller said.

New Business Comes in, But Falters

New restaurants had opened around the mushroom-shaped, concrete stadium, envisioning big business. Basements were cleared out and hundreds of tables and chairs brought in. Trouble was, the steady Kingdome tenants, the Mariners and Seahawks, didn't win nearly enough to pull in the overflow dining crowds anticipated,

particularly the woebegone baseball team, putting these hopeful eating establishments in peril or out of business.

SoDo was emblazoned all over the old Sears Building at the highest point of Seattle's biggest structure. It was stamped on green street signs that greeted people entering the area from all directions. But it wasn't until the Mariners put their own

One of the signs greeting people as they enter SoDo. This one is at the south end of 1st Avenue South.

The Mayor of SoDo

He's a short, gray-haired man in his 70s, a marketing director for a company that makes industrial heating elements. He's a University of Washington alumnus, and briefly a Huskies football player. He's a descendent of Seattle's pioneering Mercer family.

If there was one, Mike Peringer also could be the mayor of SoDo, if not hold higher office in the city's industrial district. "I joke with people that I'm the king of SoDo," Peringer said.

What's certain is others have been there longer and hold a greater financial stake in the area, but no one has been more of a SoDo caretaker than Peringer. He helped found the SoDo Business Association in 1991, giving the neighborhood more of a voice in Seattle, and has been its president ever since.

Mike Perringer is often referred to as the "Mayor of SoDo" after founding the SoDo Business Association in 1991.

SoDo Business Association Logo

He led a drive to rid the area of some of its worst visual blight, a graffiti-filled corridor running down the middle of SoDo, and wound up creating ArtWorks, an organization that allows at-risk kids the opportunity to express themselves artistically in a public fashion.

And he wrote a book about it, "Good Kids: the Story of ArtWorks," describing how 5,000 teenagers had completed

1,500 murals, many of them hanging permanently throughout the Northwest, and received many community awards along the way.

Joining Process Heating Company at 2732 3rd Avenue South in the early 1980s, Peringer was one of SoDo's many concerned tenants who had grown weary of burglaries and other petty crimes plaguing their streets. So they called for a meeting with then Seattle police chief Patrick Fitzsimons. A 7 a.m. gathering at the Rainier Brewery on a cold, wet morning surprisingly drew 500 people. Fitzsimons suggested the formation of a business association. Everyone looked to Peringer.

"We had a public safety problem, and one thing led to another, and that's how it happened," Peringer said. "They asked me to take charge of things."

In 1995, Peringer formed ArtWorks, another civic entity borne out of frustration. The middle of SoDo needed to be cleaned up. The city provided a grant to fund the effort. That first year, 750 teens (ages 13 to 17) from the King County juvenile system were enlisted to work on 23 murals that would replace and deter graffiti. Later, these kids produced 500 panels that surrounded the Qwest Field construction site. Process Heating even received a mural.

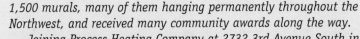

Originated by Mike Perringer, ArtWorks helps keep kids busy while beautifying Seattle and SoDo.

ArtWorks is now run out of the basement of a SoDo building at 923 South Bayview Street, keeping kids preoccupied in a productive manner and giving the industrial area and other neighborhoods a facelift.

Behind it all is Peringer, a man with a tireless devotion to SoDo and the track record to prove it. "Mike is one of the most enthusiastic people I know, not just for ArtWorks, but for all things in SoDo," said Jesse Brown, one of those at-risk kids who later became an ArtWorks artistic director. "He can get a lot of people involved."

Normally drab traffic-signal control boxes around the city are a lot more colorful now thanks to ArtWorks.

spin on SoDo that everyone climbed on board with Stagen's trademark name, make that Scigliano's creation, no, make that Miller's idea.

Refuse to Confuse

In 2000, well after the commercial real estate developers had ignored the strident opposition to their building birthmark, more brain power sat in a room and put creativity to the test, struggling to find just the right message. After all, the Mariners needed a season slogan. "Refuse to Lose" was already used. So was "You Gotta Love These Guys." The marketing hook this time was outdoor baseball. Newly constructed Safeco Field would be playing its first full season in the open air, and the new slogan had to say neighborhood, Seattle summer nights, fresh air. It was all of that, and foremost something catchy.

The Copacino+Fujikado advertising agency in Seattle had worked annually with the team since 1990 and was entrusted with finding the proper catchphrase. It took awhile for anyone to come up with something suitable, longer than usual actually. Leave it to yet another East Coast transplant to frame not only the Mariners' competitive mindset, but solve a geographic dilemma that now stretched for more than 100 years. Steve Cunetta was the ad agency's creative mind, working in tandem with senior partner Jim Copacino, whose name comes first on the company letterhead. Cunetta was the guy who finally got Seattle to pay attention and take SoDo seriously.

Every day on his way to work, Cunetta drove past that green-and-white sign on First Avenue South and Royal Brougham Way that proclaimed "WELCOME TO SODO" in big capital letters. What it meant didn't immediately register with him, either.

"I would pass by those signs and say, 'Really, is that the real estate agent's name?'" Cunetta wisecracked. "I had never heard anyone refer to (the area) like that. But being a baseball fan, there's magic where a team plays in town."

New York had Soho and its Bronx Bombers. Denver had LoDo and its Rockies. Why not SoDo for the Mariners? But there had to be more to it than that. Cunetta randomly settled on "SoDo Mojo." He mixed location with a word that meant magic spell, charm or hex.

"Like the term SoDo, 'mojo' at the time was not as ubiquitous as it is now," Cunetta said. "It had been used as a jazz word. It didn't occur to me that it was a big word in Mike Meyers' 'Austin Powers' movie. To me, it was a word used by the Doors. To me, it made sense, that 'SoDo Mojo' was a description of Mariners baseball, when magic and Mariners baseball happen in that part of town."

While fans weren't exactly sure what the latest slogan described and initially voiced that uncertainty, baseball team officials were thrilled when Cunetta and Copacino unveiled the distinctive phrase.

"I saw it and leaped out of my chair and ran over and hugged those two guys," said Kevin Martinez, Mariners vice president of marketing. "It doesn't mean anything, but I love it. It defines what the ballpark is."

"SoDo Mojo" caught on throughout the city as the baseball team won 91 games and entered postseason play, advancing as far as the American League Championship Series before being eliminated. SoDo became an official Seattle destination and not just a rallying cry, joining other, though much smaller, SoDos that had been established in Phoenix and Orlando. Even after the Kingdome was demolished in 2000, making way for Qwest Field, the name remained intact. It now meant

South of Downtown.

"I actually was a bit surprised how few people here knew the area," Cunetta recollected. "It was not called the Industrial Area anymore. I think city neighborhoods should have some romance and reflect something special about them. I'm sure it would have happened without our slogan. But if it happened in a small way because of our slogan, I'm quite pleased about that. I also like the fact they were able to demolish the Kingdome and able to retain the name. I find that fascinating."

Looks Like It's Stuck – the Scoreboard Says So

While the Mariners commission a new slogan each season, "SoDo Mojo" still appears nightly nearly a decade later on the video screen during home games at Safeco Field, a permanent part of the team lexicon, not to mention plastered on the back of car and truck windows and

bumpers for perpetuity, or at least until they wear off.

Eventually, the large, red SoDo signs were removed from the old Sears Building once Starbucks moved in and set up its corporate headquarters, requiring its own green-and-white crowned mermaid logos be put on display. Three of the displaced SoDo signs now are fastened to nearby buildings, facing east and west on top of a warehouse and south on the wall of a parking garage on 4th Avenue South. One sign remains in storage, ready to come out when a suitable place can be found for it.

"It's nice to have a name to put to something," said

"To me, it made sense, that 'SoDo Mojo' was a description of Mariners baseball, when magic and Mariners baseball happen in that part of town."

Steve Cunetta

Some businesses have adopted SoDo in their names - SoDo Pop recording studio, SoDo Granite and Stone Company, SoDo Deli, the 400-member SoDo Business Association, Showbox SoDo, and SoDo Pizza.

Anna Tucci-Ringstad, whose family owns Italia Imports Inc., a distributor of Italian-based LaVazza Coffee and located on South Spokane Street. "We like the name because it's easier to give directions to people bringing a container to us."

Said Miller, who was the original SoDo proponent, "In the old days, I used to take my kids there and people would say, 'Why would you do that? It's so awful there.' Not now."

The neighborhood isn't hurting for constant SoDo reminders. There is a new SoDo Commerce Building, SoDo Deli,

SoDo Pop recording studio, SoDo Granite and Stone Company, SoDo Park, SoDo Pizza, Showbox SoDo, SoDo Builders, www.shopsodo.com and a 400-member SoDo Business Association for namesake offerings.

Whereas it was once an unidentifiable and often ignored section of Seattle, people now comfortably call it by its proper name, affording the area a fair measure of respect. They even tend to get a little carried away at times.

"Any thought of naming it SoDo Field rather than Safeco Field?" Scigliano wanted to know.

A street-level view of Safeco Field's main entrance off 1st Avenue South and Edgar Martinez Way.

SoDo's Earthquakes

The ground starts to shake. The ground starts to swirl. The ground starts to sink like quicksand. If waiting out an earthquake in seismically active Seattle isn't bad enough, try doing it in the SoDo District, in which nearly all buildings rest atop highly unstable landfill, some up to 90 to 95 feet deep. It's a ride like none that Disneyland can provide.

"Everything is like Jello when it happens," said Tom "Tully" O'Keefe, founder of Tully's Coffee, of the SoDo District west of Airport Way South, the dividing line for hard pan and fill.

"It's like pudding during a quake," said Warren D. Cochrane, retired Millwork Supply owner.

There have been three major earthquakes in Seattle – a 7.1 Richter scale jolt in 1949, 6.5 in 1965 and 6.8 in 2001 – and during each nerve-wracking experience SoDo has been put in a blender and shaken like no other neighborhood.

Everyone agrees the most recent quake was the most disruptive for the district, pancaking one SoDo building and seriously damaging others to the point they were subjected to major repairs or torn down. Cracks in walls and floors remain visible today in businesses throughout the industrial area, caused by those attention-getting Mother Nature reminders.

"We ran for the door, which was probably stupid, and we could see the wires outside flapping back and forth," said Rex Holt, former owner of Peat Belting Company, who waited out the 2001 Nisqually earthquake with an office assistant. "She was white as a ghost. The building went a foot and a half back and forth during the quake. We stood there and watched the front of Sears (now the Starbucks Center) fall off."

Peat Belting, a 102-year SoDo occupant, sank seven feet into the unstable soil. The business was sold and moved to the suburbs. Peat's former 2430 1st Avenue South site is now a gravel parking lot.

Millwork Supply's Cochrane is one of the few people with first-hand knowledge of all three quakes that have virtually turned SoDo upside down. In 1949, one of the company's millworkers was unaccounted for following the noon-time shaker that hit the neighborhood as hard as any in Seattle and required military patrols afterward.

As for that Millwork Supply employee, he was found in the basement of one of the company's two buildings at 2225 1st Avenue South, uninjured and fascinated by the liquid-like ground beneath him, disinterested in running to safety.

"He saw a sinkhole developing and he was dip-sticking it with a 20-foot piece of molding, and he kept going down and couldn't hit anything," Cochrane said. "He was hypnotized by it. He kept getting a longer stick. It didn't matter that he might have been in danger."

In 1965, SoDo took a huge hit when the 7:28 a.m. quake struck. A man was killed by falling building debris on South King Street. Two more people died at the Fisher Flour Mill on Harbor Island from falling timber. A 50,000-gallon water tank at Fisher toppled and burst. A thousand barrels of beer were spilled at the Rainier Brewery. A car was crushed by falling bricks at 1731 1st Avenue South, yet somehow the occupants, a young couple, survived.

The 2001 quake again mistreated SoDo more than anywhere else in the city. The newly remodeled Starbucks Center at 2401 Utah Avenue South suffered $65.5 million worth of damage, forcing another remodel. Esquin Wine Merchants at 2700 4th Avenue South had 1,000 bottles shatter and its contents flood the store. The Seattle Chocolate Company at 1962 1st Avenue South suffered so much damage it had to move to the suburbs.

At O.B. Williams, a mill-working business at 1939 1st Avenue South, water shot up through the street. Lumber was tossed around inside. Cabinets fell over. Most amazing, a thick, 6x6 basement support beam totally disappeared into the soupy ground and was never found.

At nearby Millwork Supply, the damage from the most recent earthquake was eerily similar to the previous temblors that had come through the area 36 and 52 years earlier. The same support beam sank six inches into the basement soil. The same huge bulge showed up in the same place in the basement floor. The upper floors sagged in all the same places. The basement perched over the high water table was flooded again by the high water table.

see how elastic the property could be during a huge earthquake.

The building shook. A fax machine flipped over. Cabinets spilled. The warehouse had damage that required retrofitting.

There was one image that is etched in the minds of onlookers. "My brother [and company president] Stewart saw big trucks in the air," said vice president Scott Soules.

SoDo's O.B Williams and Millwork Supply, always friendly mill-working rivals and located only a block apart on the same street, had suffered similar damage. They huddled on how to put everything back as it once was, on how to reinforce those worrisome floors. They have it down to an earthquake science now.

"We used a 20-ton bottle jack to lift it up," Cochrane said. "The building creaked and moaned and cracked. It was like being in a mine."

Over at Transfer Systems and Storage, a trucking company built on former tideland, the business owners got to

As noted in these three photos, wine bottles face a grim future during an earthquake. In the 2001 Nisqually quake, SoDo's Esquin Wine lost 3,600 bottles of wine. Owner Chuck LeFevre said he was dodging the bottles, which became dangerous projectiles during the quake.

CHAPTER SEVEN - NAME THAT TIDEFLAT

An aerial view of the Seahawks' home field looking north over downtown Seattle.

Safeco Field and Qwest Field rise together majestically out of the north end of the SoDo District, dressing up the otherwise plain-looking and low-slung industrial area with their glistening new-age designs. They offer a billion dollars worth of 21st Century pro sports stadiums that come with all of the latest amenities. Foremost among these is the engineering marvel that is Safeco's retractable roof, one that allows baseball to be played, rain or shine.

The respective facilities, which are separated only by a convention center and a four-lane street, rest on sporting graveyards: Qwest Field, home to the Seattle Seahawks and Seattle Sounders, occupies ground that formerly housed the Kingdome, a concrete mushroom of a building that was declared outdated and imploded in 2000; Safeco Field, headquarters for the Seattle Mariners, sits on land once earmarked for a multi-use NBA and NHL arena proposed by the Ackerley family, former owners of the Seattle Sonics, but financing obstacles squelched that effort, leading to the ballpark.

These two stadium properties were previously used for a railyard that eventually was neglected and went unused for nearly two decades, and original tideflats that were filled in. Today, they represent a significant rebirth and respect for SoDo, a name which, of course, was crafted as a neighborhood designation for South of the Dome and now means South of Downtown.

"The mistake some cities have made is they put stadiums in remote locations and surround them with parking lots," said Tod Leiweke, Seahawks chief executive officer. "The impact a city can have by bringing stadiums to urban areas is in retail opportunities and jobs, and that gets lost. These stadiums are incredibly well-sited."

Fields of Dreams

Hired before the 2009 season, Mariners' manager Don Wakamatsu has been a long-time visitor to SoDo and a nearby Pioneer Square resident since joining the franchise. He's seen welcome changes in the working-class neighborhood that employs him. "I played a lot of minor

> "The mistake some cities have made is they put stadiums in remote locations and surround them with parking lots. The impact a city can have by bringing stadiums to urban areas is in retail opportunities and jobs, and that gets lost. These stadiums are incredibly well-sited."
>
> Tod Leiweke

One consideration to address Seattle's sports stadiums needs was this $15 million proposal in 1963 for a floating stadium in Elliott Bay.

league baseball and I would see cities about to become abandoned and become suburb cities," Wakamatsu said. "I see reinvigoration here (in SoDo), just like what's happened in Phoenix."

How this once sleepy industrial area became the center of Seattle's pro sports universe wasn't all that complicated or pretty: It was done by default. In 1959, the late Dave Cohn, who turned the uptown Metropolitan Grill into a dining institution, suggested

rather loudly that the city needed a multi-purpose pro sports stadium and started a movement to obtain one. A World's Fair was coming and business was thriving, and civic-minded people such as Cohn were convinced Seattle should become major league in every way. Yet this particular stadium dream of his wouldn't be realized for another 17 years, requiring the introduction of three bond drives (two failed) and inspection of roughly 206 sites (205 rejected).

The original suggestion was to build a stadium midway between Seattle and Tacoma. A lot of lobbying also was done to put it in Kent, near the Pacific Raceways auto track; in Renton, east of the Longacres horseracing track; in Bellevue, on a bare field near Northrup Way; in Factoria, near the busy intersection of Interstates 90 and 405; in Federal Way, near its trademark shopping center; alongside Lake Union, replacing a U.S. Navy training center; in Lynnwood,

IT'S GOING TO BE A **HIT**

PILOTS

OFFICIAL

SCOREBOOK

35¢

APRIL 1969

This 1969 program for the Seattle Pilots included a fanciful illustration of a future "Kingdome." Above the drawing is the caption: "Artist's conception of Seattle's forty-million-dollar domed stadium."

Johnny (No. 3) & Eddie (No. 4) O'Brien.

alongside Interstate 5; and in South Park and Riverton, both industrial areas located farther south than SoDo.

Most creative was a 1963 proposal to build a floating, 70,000-seat stadium in Elliott Bay, at the foot of West Harrison Street, not far from the World's Fair grounds. If approved, the sports complex would have been constructed on pontoons, similar to what holds up the city's two Lake Washington floating bridges. Plenty of moorage was planned

for this unique stadium idea, allowing fans to travel to games by boat. Other far-reaching deals were made that didn't come to fruition.

Shooting for the Center – Initially Anyway

A Seattle Center site, however, was by far the most popular among politicians and fans. Pegged for the intersection of Mercer Street and 5th Avenue North, the stadium was headed for property with

Seattle University coach Al Brightman between Eddie and Johnny O'Brien.

a decided baseball history. The site once housed a Pacific Coast League ballpark from 1903 to 1906, and was situated across the street from space that once held Civic Field, a multi-purpose ballpark that serviced PCL teams from 1932 to 1938. Memorial Stadium, the replacement for Civic Field and used mostly for high school sporting events, would have been razed to make room.

City officials gave the Seattle Center site its blessing, and Metro bus barn property was purchased. Stadium core-drilling and surveying work began in earnest in 1970.

"I was sold on it because (Sen.) Warren Magnuson agreed to have the Bay Freeway done if the stadium was done there," said Johnny O'Brien, a stadium site-selection committee member and former big-league baseball player, referring to a proposed freeway link-up that would have connected the Alaskan Way Viaduct to Interstate 5 via Mercer Street. "That would have relieved all that traffic mess back then."

Opponents, however, held up the Seattle Center site with court challenges and killed it with a public vote. People felt their residential neighborhoods would have been compromised by noise and traffic. Local activist Frank Ruano and others fought this stadium deal simply for the sport of it. Political careers were ruined by the stalemate. Another American League franchise, the Seattle Pilots, was lost because of the delays.

Inching Toward SoDo

South Park was given strong consideration until labor groups opposed it, bemoaning the potential loss of industrial land and Duwamish Waterway development. Another downtown site, planned for a hillside at 5th Avenue and Yesler Way, was also rejected.

As a last resort, the 35.9-acre King Street site in north SoDo was proposed near the end of 1971. There now was a feeling of a stadium do-or-die for everyone involved. For a change, no one legally tried to tear apart this idea, though then Mayor Wes Uhlman admitted a preference for replacing Sicks' Stadium, an abandoned minor-league ballpark in Rainier Valley, with the controversial project. International District supporters put a curse on the

Doc Maynard

SoDo Skatepark

It sits directly beneath State Route 99, hidden from view. It provides all sorts of elevation changes and intricate jumps just as the congested highway overhead begins to flatten out. This is the Marginal Way Skatepark, originally a renegade operation but now an accepted part of the SoDo landscape.

Built without permission in 2005, this skating outlet has grown into a popular hangout that has acrobats from all over the city doing their thing.

"We started building a little spot and nobody seemed to notice," said Tim Demmon, a Seattle Web and video producer, skateboarder and park founder. "Word was the city was going to demolish it, but we got some really good press, had allies in city government and other skateboard advocates, and it gave us a reprieve."

The city offered the skatepark its blessing as long as another use for the property didn't emerge at South Hanford Street and East Marginal Way. It likely was decided that this was a much healthier alternative than offered by the previous tenants, who numbered

The Marginal Way Skatepark provides a creative way to utilize unusable land.

transients, heroin users and prostitutes.

The skateboard park resembles an elaborate set of swimming pool walls, dressed up by some intricate mural artwork. Two of five sections remain unfinished, needing donations to move ahead. Stacked cement blocks that have a huge Seahawks logo painted across them provide privacy from busy East Marginal Way South and a Port of Seattle container yard.

Demmon, who founded the park – Seattle's first under cover – with fellow skaters Dan Barnett and Shawn Bishop, modeled it after Portland's Burnside Bridge Skatepark. It's a DIY, or do-it-yourself, as Demmon and his fellow skaters rely on donations of materials, cash and labor to keep the place expanding. Pearl Jam guitarist Jeff Ament, himself a skater, provided $4,000 to the cause. Local rock clubs have held benefits to raise funds.

Crews of 30 to 40 people work on upgrading the park. Skaters of all ages and proficiency are welcome. Bicycles and graffiti are highly discouraged.

"We are truly skater-built, skater-owned and a skater-run skatepark," said Demmon, whose group has its own website at www.marginalwayskatepark.org and is seeking non-profit status.

King Street stadium plan, fearing their own neighborhood infringement. New stadium construction at the King Street property began in 1973.

"They just came flying in at the end," said O'Brien, unable to determine the exact proponent of the King Street site. "There was no resistance to it, because there was no resistance around it. It was just an old, abandoned yard. I'm not sure who found it. The railroad might have offered it."

The King County domed stadium would become the

> "They just came flying in at the end. There was no resistance to it, because there was no resistance around it. It was just an old, abandoned yard. I'm not sure who found it. The railroad might have offered it."
>
> Johnny O'Brien

On March 26, 2000, the Kingdome was reduced to rubble in 16.8 seconds after 4,450 pounds of dynamite were detonated, with the collapse of the 25-ton roof sending a huge cloud of dust over parts of Pioneer Square and SoDo. Photo a copyright of Ben VanHouten.

Kingdome, with efforts resisted to name it Doc Maynard Stadium, after the notable Seattle pioneer. A few surrounding small businesses were uprooted. A powerhouse, tracks, train scale, yard station and cranes were removed from the Burlington-Northern property. The stadium would take three years to complete.

We've Heard this Before

Curiously, a 1972 stadium impact study commissioned by King County declared that residential options for the industrial area would be adversely affected, with noise, air pollution and added vehicle and pedestrian traffic providing negative sociological consequences. Nearly four decades later, city studies and resulting zoning restrictions prohibited SoDo from seeking residential buildings, intimating there would be . . . negative sociological consequences.

Decades later, two of Seattle's richest men, Microsoft co-founders Bill Gates and Paul Allen, were allowed to build projects either on or near the much-debated Seattle Center stadium site at Mercer Street and 5th Avenue North, with virtually no opposition. On the exact location, the Gates Foundation will open its huge philanthropic campus in 2011; Allen's quirky Experience Music Project has been in operation across the street since 2000.

After all of the nasty stadium battles had been waged, the Kingdome finally opened on March 27, 1976, and hosted the Seahawks, Mariners, Sonics and Sounders over its lifetime. It was in operation a day short of 24 years before it was blown up on March 26, 2000. The building was reduced to rubble in 16.8 seconds after 4,450 pounds of dynamite were detonated, with the collapse of the 25-ton roof sending a huge cloud of dust over parts of Pioneer Square and SoDo. Fans were permitted to haul off concrete souvenirs. The building had served its purpose, landing Seattle franchises in each of the three most prominent pro sports, and now it had disappeared with the flick of a switch, making way for something new.

The Safeco Field dugouts sit just four feet above the water level, and sometimes flood. When the 2001 Nisqually earthquake hit there were fears an underground tsunami might be unleashed through the fill and create problems, but nothing happened. Finding a stream running beneath the property, Safeco groundskeepers tried to think green and recycle the encroaching water. They succeeded only in killing some of the grass field because the water was too salty.

Exploring the Options

With the Kingdome nearing the end of its short lifespan, the Ackerley family sold 12.59 acres it had purchased across the street in SoDo for an 18,000-seat basketball and hockey arena. Adequate financing never materialized, nor did an NHL expansion franchise, forcing the Sonics' owners to put the property back on the market.

Rick Osterhout, a senior vice president for GVA Kidder Mathews, brokered the real-estate deal that put the site in the hands of King County and cleared the way for Safeco Field. A dirt parking lot for Kingdome events had been among its previous uses.

"It was half-financed and half-cash down, and the county guy freaked out," Osterhout recalled of the negotiations. "Home Depot was looking at it. The county got the land, but they were kicking and screaming the whole way. They paid $19.61 per square foot for dirt. It's worth $150 per square foot now. They were thinking it was super-expensive and it was a premium buy."

The 19½-acre Ackerley site, including supportive land acquisitions, was chosen – after more agonizing public discussions – as the Safeco Field site over the 12-acre north parking lot and 15½-acre south parking lot of the Kingdome. Twenty garment businesses, employing 663 people, were displaced, foremost the C.C. Filson Company.

Moving In, Moving Out

Filson, an outdoor-clothing outfitter and Seattle business staple since 1897, moved its factory to SoDo in 1985, to a 1246 1st Avenue South location, after it was uprooted by downtown condominium, office and restaurant expansion, and now it was being asked to move again. The beleaguered retailer took this battle to the state Supreme Court to no avail, ultimately landing at its current location at 1555 4th Avenue South.

Safeco Field and the vacated Kingdome stood side by side for nine months before the latter was blown to pieces. Qwest Field, originally called Seahawks Stadium, opened two years later on the Kingdome site, built on 1,700 pilings driven 50 to 70 feet into the former tideflats. Allen, the Microsoft founder-turned-Seahawks' owner, made the project happen by paying for a statewide election that barely passed yet supplied the necessary tax-generated funds to supplement his guaranteed portion of the building cost.

"I just think it's worked well, and it's worked well with us being adjacent to the Seahawks," said Chuck Armstrong, Mariners president and chief operating officer, a proponent of stadium districts. "It works well in Kansas City, where the Royals and Chiefs share a parking lot. Baltimore's Camden Yards and the Ravens' stadium have worked out well. So has Cleveland with Jacobs Park and its football stadium around the lake. In Tampa, if the Rays had their park near the football stadium, it would be much more successful."

The Pyramid Ale House

SoDo's Tideflats in the Dugouts

The SoDo quibbles for the Mariners have been minor, with the high water table always a slight cause for concern. The Safeco Field dugouts sit just four feet above the water level, and sometimes flood. When the 2001 Nisqually earthquake hit there were fears an underground tsunami might be unleashed through the fill and create problems, but nothing happened. Finding a stream running beneath the property, Safeco groundskeepers tried to think green and recycle the encroaching water. They succeeded only in killing some of the grass field because the water was too salty.

Location, Location, Location

This centralized stadium district appeals to most SoDo people, business owners such as Paul Vetters, who operates nearby Greenlake Cabinet at 2224 1st Avenue South.

Parking is a problem for him and his customers, but the business exposure has been unbeatable. "This is the greatest place for me," Vetters said. "When the Mariners have a game, people walk by. When the Seahawks have a game, people walk by. Starbucks people walk by. When Starbucks moved here, this was the place to move. I knew once they put in the Mariners stadium, this was the place to do business."

However, Bill Oseran, owner of Seattle Textile at 3434 2nd Avenue South, is not nearly as thrilled by the constant infusion of sports fans regularly bogging down SoDo streets. "Sixty thousand people come to a game, and what am I supposed to do? Go to a business meeting?" Oseran complained. "You can't do anything when there's a baseball game, especially a day baseball game. I'm a long way away, and I still can't get a truck in here."

SoDo Sex Guy

Seth Warshavsky was this Internet pioneer, the only one making millions in the early days of cyberspace, building an absolute fortune with virtual pornography. He told this story over and over again to the mainstream media, from the Wall Street Journal to Rolling Stone.

A short, brash young guy and supposedly a former Bellevue High School student, Warshavsky boasted that he was raking in $50 million in yearly revenues from 100,000 subscribers, simply by allowing them to watch naked women cavort around a SoDo warehouse in front of a camera.

Truth was a lot of what he said was a sham. He had cashed in on a celebrity sex tape independent of his main venture, but otherwise struggled to make money with his website, Internet Entertainment Group.

"He made four million off the Pamela Anderson tape," said Seattle attorney Eric Blank, Warshavsky's legal counsel on occasion. "Everything else was a loser."

Warshavsky claimed to have more than a 1,000 websites streaming his porn videos. In reality, it was 14. Everything was a distortion to anyone who came around with a news camera or a notebook.

"It was how to fool the news media, end of story," Blank said. "He didn't have these adult erotica film rooms they said he had. When the news media came around, he'd hire girls off the street and prop them up. He got away with so many extraordinary lies that nobody checked."

Warshavsky had some people believing he had studios in this huge, unmarked warehouse on 1st Avenue South. He was actually working up the street in SoDo, briefly renting an upstairs floor at the Pyramid Brewery at 1201 1st Avenue South, and facing eviction because his girls supposedly took showers that lasted so long water dripped down into the tap room.

"You really never lose," Warshavsky insisted in a 1997 Wired magazine article, always spreading untruths. "It's cheaper to produce than mainstream content and it's easier to sell."

By 2001, this new-age Larry Flynt appeared to be nothing more than an extra-greedy entrepreneur, facing grand jury investigations and outstanding bench warrants. There were claims of credit card fraud and income tax evasion, that he purposely had double- and triple-billed customers, that he owed creditors and employees. There were reports the FBI and IRS were combing through his business practices.

One of Warshavsky's last public appearances in Seattle came on May 10, 2001, when he showed up for a federal court appearance, apologized to the judge for his reclusiveness, posted bond and was released on personal recognizance. He chose to turn his back on his legal problems and run.

Warshavky fled the country to Bangkok, Thailand. The fugitive is said to be possibly dabbling in the phone sex industry, something he did before creating his Internet site.

There also have been reports he lives on a 500-acre estate. Again, lies seem to follow this scammer wherever he goes.

"It's a decent place, but it's not a compound," Blank said.

Where Can a Fan Get a Drink Around Here?

While the industrial neighborhood has experienced steady stadium expansion – three arenas over a mere three-plus decades, the surrounding area has been slow to keep up with service-related amenities. Kingdome fans largely were forced to frequent Pioneer Square restaurants and bars. There are only four SoDo drinking establishments now operating in the immediate vicinity of Safeco and Qwest: the Pyramid Alehouse and Brewery at 1201 1st Avenue South, the Hawks Nest Bar and Grill at 1028 1st Avenue South, Sluggers Bar and Grill at 538 1st Avenue South, and the newer Elysian Fields at 542 1st Avenue South.

"The big mistake is there has been no plan to improve the surrounding areas of the stadiums," pointed out Frank Firmani, developer and former SoDo business owner. "You still have a carpet dealer next to the baseball stadium. It's not Denver."

A futuristic vision for the redevelopment of the waterfront near SoDo.

In 1988, shortly before Seattle's industrial district was christened SoDo, Denver started remaking the northwest corner of its downtown region, calling it LoDo, for Lower Downtown. Restaurants and bars now surround the city's two stadiums, Coors Field and the Pepsi Center, as do artist lofts and historical buildings such as Union Station have been updated.

Changes in the Air?

"I've studied San Diego's Petco Park, Bell Park in San Francisco and Coors Field in Denver, and those are three great examples of what one stadium has done to an area, and the city has embraced it," Seattle developer Greg Smith said. "Those cities created a community around their stadiums, and that hasn't happened here. Let's not be leapfrogged by other cities, which we have. Let's bring ourselves to be the most competitive. Let's celebrate those stadiums."

The Mariners, however, have tried to slow some of the neighborhood progress. They have been among SoDo tenants who have fought the city acceptance of a strip club near Safeco Field. Ironically, the industrial area supported

Interior view of King Street Station restoration.

Exterior view of King Street Station restoration.

a well-known topless joint, Budnicks, on the stadium site before the Kingdome was built.

"We are a family-nature business," the Mariners' Armstrong said. "This is a Mountain-Sound 'green belt,' that includes our plaza, with a number of kids and families, and it's a real concern. We complained. We should be thought of as a park and protected."

No Places to Live – Yet

SoDo residential offerings remain limited and almost all confined to the immediate stadium area, not counting the army of camper trucks arbitrarily parked throughout the industrial district. Within short walking distance of the two stadiums' gates are the 116-unit Florentine Condominiums at 536 1st Avenue South, 30 artist lofts in the Bemis Building at 55 South Atlantic Street and the 211-room Sta-

dium Silver Cloud at 1046 1st Avenue South. The exception comes at the southern end of SoDo, where there are 20 artist lofts in the Old Rainier Brewery at 3100 Airport Way South, and 18 artist lofts in the multi-colored Sunny Arms Artist Cooperative – the former Sunny Jim peanut butter factory at 707 South Snoqualmie Street and rebuilt after a 1997 fire.

Others suggest that SoDo is on the verge of

remaking itself, that stadium accessories are not that far off. "People ask me is this the best and biggest use?" the Seahawks' Leiweke said. "These are two stadiums where it incidentally came true and all promises have been upheld. SoDo was sort of a long, forgotten property. Now you can see the balance of the city is changing, and SoDo is going to change, too. You're going to see it develop, be residential, retail and commercial. Now people are having the courage to dream about things. It's kind of cool to see."

"With the viaduct coming down and the tunnel coming in, I think over the next six to seven years there's going to be a major transformation here," the Mariners' Armstrong said.

How About Some Roundball – Again?

A future addition to SoDo that multiple development groups have been mulling, even with the Sonics uprooted

> "If you ever wanted to build a basketball arena, the best place would be south of Safeco. You'd have parking for all three stadiums, near the off-ramps. It's perfect place to build a stadium. They could have all three there."
>
> Mick McCoy

to Oklahoma City and turned into the Thunder, is a third pro sports facility bent on bringing the NBA back to Seattle. Sites that have been privately or publicly discussed for a possible basketball arena have included piers 46-47, Qwest Field's north lot (again), the United Warehouse Company at 1750 Occidental Avenue South next door to the Mariners' parking garage, and MacMillan-Piper Inc. at 1762 6th Avenue South, which might be news to some of those tenants.

A basketball arena has been a regular topic of conversation among those who frequent the neighborhood. After all, SoDo already houses two huge pro stadiums, why not add a third?

"If you ever wanted to build a basketball arena, the best place would be south of Safeco," said Mick McCoy, co-owner of O.B. Williams mill-working company. "You'd have parking for all three stadiums, near the off-ramps. It's perfect place to build a

stadium. They could have all three there."

"We'll bring the NBA back," said Tom "Tully" O'Keefe, owner of Tully's Coffee. "My prediction is the (Portland) Trail Blazers will move here. We'll build an arena in the north parking lot of Qwest Field. We'll have a wonderful facility and atmosphere."

Downtown Freddy Brown's Idea

Former Sonics guard Fred Brown and public relations' executive Dave Bean have explored arena possibilities in SoDo, encouraging former Sonics coach Bill Russell to join them in a show of public support. Developers Frank Stagen and Greg Smith have put ideas on the table for waterfront housing and stadium-area development. Microsoft chief executive officer Steve Ballmer and developer Matt Griffin also are looking, continuously plotting ways to bring the NBA back to the city.

In its favor is a SoDo District that has flourished as a partner to professional sports, an industrial area that once gladly welcomed the Kingdome when others were unwilling or unable. Whereas people might have doubted the staying power of SoDo, the neighborhood has a certifiable track record when it comes to mixing with stadiums and upgrading them. The place always has presented a hard-working environment. Now a lot of steel and cement have given it a glossy sheen, a far more handsome exterior more than three decades in the making.

Since the stadiums were built, nearby King Street Station and Union Station, servicing Amtrak and Sound Transit trains, respectively, have been restored or remodeled. There's still plenty of work to be done, but the neighborhood bar definitely was raised by the inclusion of the sports palaces.

"It was a dull, old part of town," said O'Brien, who

would later serve as a King County commissioner and Kingdome official. "I don't think too many people went down there at night. It was a dead end. In the end, putting a stadium there was a bonus. You see a much neater and cleaner area with good business going in. I think it's been a real positive in the long run. It worked."

There's certainly no doubt that the horns from passenger and freight trains that resonate during Mariners games are a ready reminder of where the stadium is located.

James Dillon and crew.

James Dillon is a building contractor by trade, a time traveler at heart. Dressed in sunglasses, yellow helmet, tan coat, gray pants and work boots – a standard-issue working-man's uniform that he makes look very cool, this bearded, middle-aged man with a Gentleman's Quarterly aura about him comes to work each day in the SoDo District and merges the past with the present.

Dillon has put his stamp on 20 SoDo properties, remodeling 17 of them. For him, this requires stripping away the outer veneer of a Depression-era building while reinforcing and preserving the guts of it. He mixes two very different worlds. While others in his profession would be more apt to put a wrecking-ball to one of these projects, then clear away the crumpled mess and start over, he carefully removes thick, classic cuts of lumber from one structure and reuses them in another, largely because building materials of such purity and elegance are hard to find. Plus it's far more cost-effective to work in this manner if you have the patience for it.

Disturbances of the Past

At the same time, this transplanted Pittsburgh native, who has a Masters degree in architecture, does not intend to get in the way of what he views as the natural evolution of Seattle's largest industrial corridor, which is to say the transformation of pricey and centralized real estate into something other than a neighborhood of old buildings and old ways of doing business. He'll preserve stuff, but only to a point.

"Over a long period of time, the solution to pollution is dilution," Dillon says, repeating – but in no way taking credit for – the mantra offered by Gershon Cohen, a nationally recognized environmentalist. "Buildings represent a certain amount of historical vein, but they hold up economic progress. They're not historical monuments."

A tour of SoDo commences, with Dillon marching up the street with a swagger, leading his hungry work crew to lunch at a nearby Vietnamese restaurant, Pho Cyclo. The street in front of this busy eatery at 2414 1st Avenue South is torn up, in many sections providing little more than a dirt surface, not unlike what was

"Over a long period of time, the solution to pollution is dilution. Buildings represent a certain amount of historical vein, but they hold up economic progress. They're not historical monuments."

James Dillon

The Gorelich/Dillon Building following a major renovation.

found here at the turn of the previous century. Historical remnants of what came next – a brick road that catered to frantic street trolley and Model T automobile traffic – are exposed in the different layers of ground excavated by the construction. This is no misguided return to the horse-and-buggy days, rather prep work on water and sewer lines in advance of waterfront tunneling that eventually will replace the Alaskan Way Viaduct and emerge above ground in SoDo.

The Pho Cyclo owner always has a full restaurant for lunch, but is losing considerable takeout business because of the lingering road work, the second such disruption within a year for him and his neighbors. A concerned Dillon offers his counsel, suggesting that customers be encouraged to drive through a back alley for their pick-up orders and that small service alterations be made: maybe a turf walkway covering or delivery window could easily be made to accommodate them.

Dillon, sort of a Pied Piper of SoDo, points to various 1st Avenue South addresses and recites their histories. B&K Tool was over there, fortunate to go out of business when it did. The owner chose to close down his company instead of giving in to higher rent. Two months later, the building B&K once occupied was flattened by the 2001 Nisqually earthquake. By making a smart business decision, the man probably was fortunate to be alive, let alone avoid a huge financial

The SoDo Coffee Clatch

Where do you find a good cup of coffee in SoDo? A more compelling question is where in the industrial district won't you find one?

This is the caffeine capital of urban America. National brands Starbucks and Tully's are headquartered here. Newcomer Stella is blended here. LaVazza is imported from Italy to the area.

"We all need quasi-industry space or industrial space," Tully's founder Tom "Tully" O'Keefe noted. "We'd all rather be close to the city. But I think there's zero influence over us coffee guys that we want to congregate. I think it is coincidence."

Starbucks headquarters now occupies the old Sears Building.

Starbucks came first, moving into a former Eddie Bauer's warehouse at 2010 Airport Way South in 1989. Within four years, the coffee company had experienced such explosive growth it was forced to move its roasting plant to Kent and start looking for bigger office space, finally moving into the old Sears and Roebuck building. The much bigger edifice at 2401 Utah Avenue South was specifically remodeled for the growing coffee giant's needs in 1997.

"I admit that I was less than enthusiastic about potentially moving to what was then a fairly dilapidated building with a terrifically un-hip reputation," Howard Schultz, Starbucks chairman, said in "Rebuilding a Legacy," a book detailing the history of the Starbucks Center. "But we were growing so fast that . . . we decided to take the plunge and at least temporarily call the former Sears warehouse our home."

Starbucks is still there, though the 2001 Nisqually earthquake would severely damage the building, requiring a second remodel and cause Schultz and his employees to do some serious scrambling. The company peaked at more than 16,000 worldwide retail stores, including a pair in SoDo, before the economy forced a significant number of closures.

Tully's followed Starbucks into SoDo, even following its coffee rival into the same warehouse on Airport Way South. With more than 100 retail stores located mostly on the West Coast, Tully's now headquarters in the former Rainier Brewery at 3100 Airport Way South and has a street-side coffee outlet there.

In 2008, Tully's sold its roasting operation to Vermont-based Green Mountain while keeping its retail business intact. The company moved its roasting plant to a larger facility Sumner, Wash., in fall 2009, but maintains its headquarters for Tully's retail operations at the old Rainier Brewery site.

Italia Imports and Exports, a distributor of Italian-roasted LaVazza coffee founded by Alfonso and Esther Tucci, moved into a former military and foundry building at 126 South Spokane Street in 1992. It's run by their daughter, Anna Tucci-Ringstad, and son, Roberto Tucci.

(continued on page 102)

Coffee concerns superseded the former Rainier Brewery.

One of James Dillon's favorite places in SoDo is the upper floor at Millwork Supply.

window, practically a museum piece, sat in the shop for the longest time before a contractor couldn't resist buying it and finding another place for it. The fading outline of an old-style pickleball court can be found on the second floor, once a passion for the first-generation and deceased Walter A. Cochrane. Antique bicycles collecting dust are stored upstairs, as well.

Dillon takes photos of everything with a cell-phone

loss. Not far from there was the Seattle Chocolate Company, a thriving SoDo business until the quake severely damaged the brick building, forcing a change in ownership and a move to Tukwila. That structure might have survived, Dillon points out, had its tar-and-gravel roof been replaced by something lighter and more shock-resistant. Instead, the heavy load above caused building walls to splay out.

SoDo's Museum of Sorts

One of Dillon's favorite stops is Millwork Supply, which can count four generations of Cochrane family members as employees and/or owners for nearly nine decades. The 2225 1st Avenue South shop has all of its original cutting knives and keeps pattern books dating back to the 1930s, which means even the oldest customer can return and get millwork repairs done without having to replace everything. An insulated, curved glass

One of Dillon's biggest SoDo Projects is at 1531 Utah Avenue South.

Stella Coffees moved their roasting facilities from this SoDo warehouse to Kent.

(continued from page 100)

"It seems like all the major coffee companies have moved here," Tucci-Ringstad said. "It seems like since we've been here that downtown Seattle is moving closer and closer to us. We like it here. It's very centralized."

Italia receives container deliveries by rail from New Jersey and then trucks the coffee to Seattle-area restaurants and cafes, and some hotels and casinos.

Stella is the relative newcomer to SoDo, an Italian-style and locally roasted coffee company that moved to Seattle from Australia in 2007. The owners are Alaskan native Rob Wilson and his Australian wife Josie Sassano-Wilson, the latter of Italian-Australian descent. Talk about a rich coffee blend.

If that wasn't enough, Wilson renamed the company, originally called Bell Café Coffees in Australia, after his sister, a California resident, for a reason that needs full explanation.

"It's the nickname for our coffee roaster, which is really old, made in 1925," Wilson explained. "My sister Stella is sort of a funny gal, really particular and fussy and hard to manage. Working on the coffee roaster is sort of the same thing."

Stella, which hopes to expand nationally once the economy settles, keeps its retail outlet and offices in downtown Seattle, but has a roasting SoDo facility at 3828 4th Avenue South that isn't hard to find. It's the place with the coffee beans spilled all around the front steps, leaving an inviting odor.

camera, no doubt preserving images for construction inspiration. A classic door-making machine sits inoperable because it's too expensive to fix, but remains on the main floor for display purposes. Two well-worn hospital gurneys are used to move materials, not bodies, from room to room. Millwork Supply handiwork is found in the most unique places.

"That's holding (Dale) Chihuly glass down in the Bellagio in Las Vegas," Kevin Cochrane said, pointing to a particular framework.

Tacked to a Millwork Supply office wall, in a hallway above the employee timecard clock, is a yellowed Department of Labor and Industries flier, kept more as a keepsake though its message still radiates. This piece of paper is dated August 28, 1923, urging safety in the workplace while quoting statistics of job-related deaths and injuries.

More Stops on the Tour

Dillon continues the tour north, past the Macrina Bakery, Martin-Smith artist lofts, O.B. Williams (another millwork company) and Outdoor Research (military clothing). He walks north until he reaches a mid-rise building under construction at 1531 Utah Avenue South, two streets removed from Safeco Field. This building is the exception to the strict zoning restrictions that govern most of SoDo, but it could become the norm. Along the way, Dillon identifies several SoDo nightclubs, marked and unmarked. The contractor in him registers disgust as he points to a crumbling Seattle Business Design building next door to the mid-rise site.

"It's the sorriest wreck I think I've seen in the area," the contractor said. "I think I've fixed all the others."

Dillon returns to the southern end of 1st Avenue South, where his most recently completed and

2962 First Avenue S.
formerly the shack

James Dillon added "Formerly the Shack" to his building at 2962 1st Avenue South to describe the decrepit condition of the building before it was refurbished.

current projects are located in a cluster. One of his remodels, housing the Renewal Window Company by Anderson, is a shiny new place that offers a prominent clue to its not-so-glorious past. Fastened across the top of the single-story building for everyone driving past to see is the full address, 2962 1st Avenue South, with the words "Formerly the Shack" spelled out on the line below it.

"It really was a shack," Dillon said. "That's me being funny."

Next door, at 2944 1st Avenue South, is another Dillon remodel with an entertainment-related history, though the place sits empty and carries no catchy outside label. Originally a foundry that opened in 1918 and was used to supply World

War I needs, the building later was owned by Moe Gorelick, a plumbing wholesale supplier and the father of contemporary jazz musician Kenny G.

Taking a Look at the Bigger Picture

Around the corner is one of Dillon's latest efforts, the SoDo Commerce Building, identified by big block letters across the top and lit up gloriously on all sides at night. It was a paper-recycling plant in the 1930s. It now is a handsome new structure, given a neo-Italian design, something Dillon saw in person that was used to give a post office in Florence architectural lifeblood.

Dillon's latest projects include buildings previously occupied by Ederer Crane, which has since moved its

manufacturing operations to Georgia, and a former horse barn that needs a lot of reconditioning, a bag of oats, all of the above. Dillon and his gregarious foreman, Jaime Blankenship, who has an American flag decal and the words "Support our Troops" fastened to his white construction helmet, oversee these projects in animated fashion. What they're doing

is progress. It's also a bare snapshot of what Dillon, this dapper and opinionated man who doesn't mind getting dirty, thinks is the neighborhood's bigger picture.

"If we can get the railroad and the Seattle Port Authority out of the area, you give up a fiefdom," Dillon pointed out of the SoDo dynamics. "Seattle could grow another million people. Will it happen? No."

A 2009 view looking north on 1st Avenue South.

Western Bridge building at 3212 Fourth Avenue South now houses a contemporary art gallery and a warehouse.

The "True" Museum

Western Bridge best amplifies the change that is overtaking SoDo in 2009. It once was the name of a contracting firm that built the Spokane Street viaduct and several overpasses on Interstates 5 and 405. Today, the name identifies a contemporary art gallery occupying a 10,000-square-foot warehouse at 3412 4th Avenue South.

The only connection between the two is Elmer James White Sr. He created Western Bridge and built the aforementioned warehouse, though the two were never connected. He later changed the name of his now Georgetown-based contracting business to Mobile Crane, because it better described the work that he did. He also sold the warehouse, which is called a step-back because it sits well off 4th Avenue South, though it carries that street address.

Since 2004, this somewhat hidden building has been occupied by an art gallery owned by Bill and Ruth True, with people more apt to get all dressed up for a Friday night opening, sip from wine glasses and inspect some new exhibit offered from the Trues' extensive personal collection, rather than perform some gritty job such as the previous tenant, a tile-cutting and showroom.

"The artwork has nothing to do with Western Bridge," said White's son, Jim. "That's just the True museum."

Diversification with a Small "D"

This is a growing trend for SoDo, which has become much more diversified, welcoming the arts and retail among others to the area while the more demanding manufacturing companies exit. Welding and fabricating shops have been supplanted by something far less involved.

"SoDo was more heavy industry before," Western Bridge director Eric Fredericksen said. "Now we have a wine importer, a Plexiglas company, a candle maker, a film crew equipment place across the way. I don't want to say boutique industries, but it's interesting."

A Hard Guy with a Soft Heart for Art

Mobile Crane, formerly Western Bridge, is located in Georgetown and run by the second-generation White, a gruff person with a long resume in heavy and complicated construction that

> *"The phone rang down here for some time because people were looking for information for showings. We were down here thinking of construction and running cranes, and those people were talking art. It was sometimes humorous and sometimes overloading. They wanted to use the name. I didn't object."*
>
> Jim White

Jim White of Mobile Crane.

stretches from coast to coast. Imagine Jim White's consternation at the steady stream of phone calls to his office from people asking about the gallery. Yet this steel man actually seemed flattered that someone wanted to preserve his family's previous business name.

"The phone rang down here for some time because people were looking for information for showings," White said. "We were down

here thinking of construction and running cranes, and those people were talking art. It was sometimes humorous and sometimes overloading. They wanted to use the name. I didn't object."

Developer Starts Small

Scott Andrews always wanted to own a warehouse. In 1994, this semi-retired Seattle dentist decided the time was right and he bought one – and another and another. Andrews ended up with six fairly inexpensive SoDo buildings, all located along 1st Avenue South. He figured this was a solid investment. There was increasing speculation that the Seattle Mariners baseball team was going to get a new home up the street, and a modern ballpark surely would increase neighborhood land values for everyone else.

"I started buying when they were giving property away," he said.

Andrews also wanted to have some fun with his

newly acquired SoDo empire. He gave each structure a personalized name. There was the K.R. Trigger Building, which was formerly a hair products supply company. The initials in the name that was fastened across the top of the building at 3201 1st Avenue South were meant to recognize his sons, Kyle and Ryan, and Trigger was the nickname given to him by a teammate for his rapid-fire shooting ability as a Roosevelt High School basketball player. The Thompson/Sykes/Bucks Building was christened for the maiden names of his mother-in-law, mother and stepmother, respectively. The Vertigo Building was named after one of his favorite Hollywood films, the Buena Vista Building after a favorite San Francisco café, and so on.

"I liked old," Andrews said. "Everything I like is old. I love everything 1920s, '30s and '40s. I love hardwood floors and big-beam ceilings."

Andrews also had a thing

105

CHAPTER NINE - NEW SODO VS. OLD SODO

McKinstry's Wellness Center

for neon signs. He installed 50 of them at one time worth $200,000 in the Trigger Building, among them Kitsap Lake Drive-In, Warshal's and Beth's Cafe signs, all classics. He had a Vertigo sign made and hung on the outside of that building, prominently displaying a falling Jimmy Stewart character. He was sued after putting up an Andrews Brothers' neon sign for his sons that mimicked the Warner Brothers logo in the film-making world, and was forced to take it down.

The Trigger Building was his flagship hangout. He installed an eight-seat movie theater plus a replica pirate ship bar purchased from a Spokane restaurant. He brought in wax figures of baseball legends Pete Rose and Ty Cobb. He donated parties for various causes and charity auctions. He invited friends over for social gatherings, able to squeeze in as many as 40 people at a time.

Earthquake Shatters Dreams

The fun lasted until the 2001 earthquake damaged one of his SoDo buildings and made Andrews rethink his real estate investments. Over the past five years, he has sold off most of his holdings, keeping only a quarter share of the Buena Vista at 3200 1st Avenue South, now known as the Herban Pottery and Patio Building. The Trigger Building mostly sits idle these days, advertising for new tenants. The Vertigo Building keeps the image of Jimmy Stewart an unmistakable SoDo landmark.

Change has sent Andrews, who teaches dentistry part-time at the University of Washington and donates his tooth-care services to a long list of assisted living centers, moving in a different business direction. He now owns 10 properties in Des Moines and its surrounding area, including a restaurant.

The New: Company's Credo – and SoDo – Lure Presidential Visit

The surprising phone call came on a Tuesday. Barack Obama would be stopping by for a visit on Thursday. The McKinstry Company, located on the southernmost tip of the SoDo District, was told to brace itself. This reputable yet unassuming mechanical contracting firm was about to land smack in the middle of a presidential election.

Ten months before the 2008 race was settled, Obama traveled to Seattle for a campaign stop, his second in the city. With an open block of time available before he would deliver a scheduled message to an overflow gathering of loyal supporters at Key Arena, the Democratic candidate asked to tour a local business deeply involved in the "green" energy movement. McKinstry was offered.

On a February morning, Obama arrived by motorcade convoy at the

5005 3rd Avenue South address, which runs down a side street, not a main thoroughfare, and is surrounded by warehouses and storage yards. He rode over SoDo's uneven and pothole-pocked roads in a jet-black sports utility vehicle equipped with tinted,

Obama was paraded through the in-house comfort areas such as the delicatessen, wine-tasting bar, combined workout gym and basketball court, and, on the rooftop, a barbecuing area and two-station, net-covered golf driving range. He took off his coat and fired up a couple of left-handed three-point shots while looking over the basketball floor that came with a huge McKinstry logo at center court that gave it a collegiate feel. If the White House didn't have one of those before, it does now.

bullet-proof windows and a thickly-shielded frame. He was accompanied by Secret Service agents, his advisors and Seattle mayor Greg Nickels in similar transportation. He was followed by a chartered bus ferrying around national media members covering his election pursuits.

The candidate was whisked through two sprawling McKinstry buildings, one holding office space, the other used for production. He seemed genuinely surprised to find this particular combination of people working so closely together in one general location, possibly thinking he would encounter only tech-minded types hunkered down in cubicles. He spent considerable time chatting up the welders and pipe-fitters.

"What he really enjoyed was the ability to go visit our shop and meet the blue-collar guys," confirmed Dave Rost, McKinstry vice president for electrical services and one of the willing tour guides.

Before he was elected as America's 44th President, Barack Obama made a campaign stop at McKinstry Company in SoDo.

Obama was shown the Knowledge Response Center, a room that seemed better suited for some secret government outpost back in Washington, D.C. It is here that McKinstry employees, surrounded by a bank of video

SoDo's Pecos Pit

Ron and Debra Wise hardly saw each other. One went to work as a paper salesman, the other a secretary. Nights together were not enough. A change was needed to fill the void.

From this sense of spousal longing, Pecos Pit BBQ was born. "He wanted us to do something together," Debra Wise said. "He was from Texas and he wanted to do barbecue."

On April 1, 1980, they opened their SoDo restaurant in a former gas service station at 2260 1st Avenue South. No fooling, the place was an instant hit.

Their menu was a simple yet tantalizing list and the same one offered today: they serve three sandwiches – Pecos beef, sliced beef and Pecos pork; side orders of link sausage and baked beans; chips and soft drinks.

"When Ron got out of school, he was a meat-cutter and he came from a family of barbecue," Debra Wise said. "He took that recipe and tweaked it to his liking, and that's how he got the sauce."

A newfound Christian couple, the Wises spent two years of planning and praying before opening the venture. After nearly settling on a Bellevue site, they leased the SoDo property from a man named

Ed Hodges, someone who was highly sympathetic to the needs of a start-up business. Hodges charged his new tenants only a few hundred dollars of monthly rent, telling them they could pay him

(continued on page 110)

Here's the crew at Pecos Pit, from left to right: Eloy Andaluz, Sara Andaluz, Stephanie Diaz, Mario Maganda, Rina Rivero and owners Debra and Ron Wise.

monitors, track the cooling, electrical and other support systems of companies nationwide that have been retrofitted by the Seattle contractor. Hundreds of miles away, these people act as quasi-building superintendents, with the ability to prevent problems or fix them with the stroke on a keyboard.

Obama was shown other energy- and cost-saving measures that McKinstry sells and uses, its various mechanical units purposely left uncovered so customers and VIP guests such as the presidential candidate can wander through the building and inspect them up close.

And at this employee-friendly company, Obama was paraded through the in-house comfort areas such as the delicatessen, wine-tasting bar, combined workout gym and basketball court, and, on the rooftop, a barbecuing area and two-station, net-covered golf driving range. He took off his coat and fired up a couple of left-handed three-point shots while looking over the basketball floor that came with a huge McKinstry logo at center court that gave it a collegiate feel. If the White House didn't have one of those before, it does now.

Obama next spoke in an open-air lounge area to McKinstry employees standing on two levels, using the moment to announce his energy plans if elected. He spoke of putting a cap on carbon emissions, of investing in energy-technology research and of setting new goals for meeting green standards. He was presented with a "jersey" cut out of sheet metal, with the words "Obama

Employees of McKinstry put together a "jersey" made of sheet metal for presidential hopeful Barack Obama when he visited in 2008.

The exterior of the McKinstry Company.

08" inscribed on it, and his customized body armor now hangs on a company wall, autographed by the man who would soon become America's 44th President. He shook hands nonstop and made a big impression on everyone by spending quality time in SoDo, even with people who still weren't going to vote for him.

"I was standing right next to him and I was reading his speech," Rost said. "Of course, I'm a Republican, but it was still pretty cool."

Real Mixed-Use

For an area of town often ignored, if not outright avoided, by Seattle's richest and most famous, an Obama visit was a reaffirmation that SoDo, even with its broken-down buildings, mangled streets and fairly visible collection of street people, should be taken seriously. Too often the neighborhood has been dismissed as a place people definitely want to skirt lest they get hemmed in on all sides by train, truck and light-rail traffic; or have their

(continued from page 108)

back once they were able to pay the regular $1,100 amount.

Ron Wise, who hails from Burkbarnett, Texas, near the Oklahoma state line, did the cooking in the back while Debra Wise, a California native who has accounting skills, worked the front counter window at Pecos Pit. The place became so popular in SoDo, serving upwards of 350 sandwiches per day, another window became necessary. On the restaurant's 25th anniversary in 2005, Ron Wise estimated they had served up 1.3 million sandwiches.

Everyone eats outside, regardless of the weather, on 19 picnic tables. The trees in the courtyard were only a few feet tall when they were planted by the Wises, who own the property now. Pecos Pit is open year-round, 11 a.m. to 4 p.m., Monday through Friday.

The Wises work just a couple days a week now, turning the operation over to a dependable crew of married couples, people who apparently want to be around each other just like their employers. All of this makes for a restaurant with lots of staying power.

"We will never sell it; it's not in our plans," said Debra Wise, one of Seattle's sunniest personalities. "We'll never retire; it's not in our plans. We've got a great crew and this is their livelihood, too."

Construction workers remodeling the Starbucks Center building used to kid that they worked "west of Pecos." That they would come from one place to eat at the other only made sense.

"In Texas they have these stands like Starbucks, on every corner," Debra Wise pointed out. "It's a good old takeout, nothing-fancy kind of place. That's what we decided to do."

vehicle suspensions tested while going almost anywhere over streets under construction or rolling like waves from the unstable tideland fill, surfaces only a skateboarder could appreciate; or experience a chance meeting with some unsavory character lurking in the shadows at night, a situation that has required some landowners to take preventative means.

"It was scary down there," said Frank Firmani, who moved his construction firm from SoDo to Ballard after a drug rehabilitation clinic was installed next door to his business. "On weekends and at night, I was always packing a .357 Magnum."

While city officials and land developers argue over how to use this unrefined and somewhat undefined section of city in the future – currently protected for industrial use by non-negotiable zoning restrictions versus given a chance to gentrify into office space and residential offerings and even

push industrial out of the neighborhood – McKinstry seemingly has the blueprint that satisfies everyone. Hundreds of people sit in airy office spaces, drawing up plans for retrofit projects, while the production guys hammer away in the shop across the street, with the exercise and food outlets providing employees all the comforts of home.

"I'll go down early on a Saturday and work out and spend most of the day there," Rost said. "A lot of community groups like our building so much they have their meetings there, like PAWS."

The McKinstry business mantra is spelled out with its own catchy acronym, DBOM, which means to design, build, operate and maintain. University of Washington graduates compose most of the executive team, including company president Dean Allen, localizing this operation. The company was created in 1960 with six plumbers working commercial and residential jobs and answering to founding partners Merrill McKinstry and George Allen, Dean's father. It evolved from there into something trend-setting, and something far-reaching, with 13 offices nationwide. Business is so good now, with annual revenues of $400 million, that McKinstry, even during a serious recession slowing down nearly everyone else, is expanding its SoDo presence by adding a third building covering 120,000 square feet and possibly up to 500 new jobs.

Obama was impressed, and he wasn't done with McKinstry, either. Two weeks before the 2008 national election was decided, he sat and made a 30-minute infomercial pushing his campaign platforms. He mentioned McKinstry by name. He surprised everyone back in SoDo a second time, following up his short-notice visit of the plant with this high-profile endorsement. The ad was shown on seven

Looking across Puget Sound from downtown Seattle; viewing one of many Washington State Ferries in the foreground with the Olympic Penninsula in the distance.

TV networks and watched by 34 million people. It made an already successful SoDo company suddenly more visible and attractive to potential customers, and the phones started ringing. There's nothing like a Presidential seal of approval to spike the company workload.

"They're retrofitting schools and office buildings to make them energy-efficient, creating jobs, saving their customers money, reducing carbon emissions and helping

end our dependence on Middle Eastern oil," Obama enthused of the SoDo company while seated in an office setting during a scripted moment before a TV camera. "As president, I'll use companies like McKinstry as models for the nation."

Obama made good on his promise and, once elected, awarded McKinstry a 10-year, $5 billion contract from the U.S. Department of Energy to retrofit federal buildings, a deal projected

to more than double the company's revenues.

SoDo, often the neglected or misunderstood Seattle neighborhood, proceeded to smile and wink at its long-time critics and take a sweeping bow after pulling an American President firmly into its corner.

And the Old . . .

The property at 915 South Walker Street sits in the shadow of Interstate 5, just

The First Costco Store

They wanted to open a wholesale store with plenty of space in an industrial area. They nearly leased property in Kent and looked at possibilities throughout Seattle. In 1983, they chose a former ship chandlery site in SoDo, at 4401 4th Avenue South.

Yet after all this careful deliberation, the owners of the first Costco store almost immediately regretted their decision.

A week after signing the lease and moving in, they found out the city was going to shut down 4th Avenue South and rebuild the bridge over the nearby railyard, a project that would take more than a year to complete and conceivably endanger Costco's success.

"Here we had this fledgling business and they were going to close the main artery," recalled Jeff Brotman, Costco chairman and co-founder. "We begged them for a delay. Give us six months, three months, whatever. I think they postponed it for a month to help us. We weren't exactly a household name."

Costco would survive these initial obstacles to become an American staple, now with 550 stores in 40 states. People had no trouble finding the flagship outlet, but not the people who were envisioned to support the store, with home – not business – owners becoming the targeted customers. The first store opened on September 15, 1983, with Brotman's father, Bernie, the owner of Seattle retail stores bearing his first name, receiving Costco card No. 1.

Business was such a success in SoDo, in fact, that Costco would replace its original 104,000-square-foot warehouse and main offices with a 154,000-square-foot building in 2005 (with its headquarters already moved to Issaquah). This would require the purchase of neighboring property owned by the Seattle School District, which had moved to the middle of SoDo.

However, the new Costco store didn't happen without another challenge.

After denying SoDo entry to other retail-minded companies, the city had made an exception and allowed this wholesaler to open its business in an area set aside for heavy industry. Now there was opposition to the Costco store expansion from people protective of the blue collar jobs. It didn't last long.

At the Manufacturing and Industrial Council of Seattle, a vote was held on whether to fight or support the store expansion. Many MIC members held up their Costco cards in an affirmative response. The SoDo-Costco relationship has worked well for everyone.

"I think the area is very vibrant," Brotman said. "It has something that's very unique in the city of Seattle. It's very central to everything in the city. It's not very far from the northern suburbs or southern suburbs. You can get there in five minutes from West Seattle or Beacon Hill. Even with out-of-the-way Magnolia, it's just 15 minutes to SoDo."

During the 2005 ribbon-cutting ceremonies for the new store, a Costco official declared that this was the company's 352nd outlet, a ready mistake. He drew a strong rebuke from co-founder Jim Sinegal, who clarified the SoDo's store permanent standing as the original in a very successful chain.

"It's not 352," Sinegal corrected. "It's oh-one and always will be."

Costco's original store opened in 1983 and was remodeled in 2005.

off busy Airport Way South. Stellar Industrial Supply and the Katwall drywall company occupy the space. A hotel, a rarity for SoDo, nearly landed there.

Landowner Bruce Eastes, a descendent of the Lee and Eastes trucking firm, proposed a four-story, 70-room hotel for the location, possibly a Holiday Inn Express. After fighting considerable public opposition to a residential offering pegged for a district zoned industrial-only, Eastes gained city approval and lined up the necessary financial backing.

Eastes gained inspiration for this project after noticing that a solitary hotel had flourished in Portland's industrial area. Why not SoDo?

"This isn't just a bunch of dirty industrial-area buildings down here," Eastes said. "We've got one of the nicest and cleanest industrial areas. I call it a commercial area. People only see the smoke stacks, grease and dirty welding. There's so much

that people do down here that others don't know about."

Ultimately, the Eastes' hotel plan was scuttled by the 9/11 terrorist actions in New York and the resulting nationwide economic fallout. His hotel financing was cut from 70 percent to 45 by his lender, too much of a drop to proceed.

In 2006, SoDo finally welcomed its first hotel to the area when the nine-story

Bennett bought a new sump pump to replace an old one that wouldn't shut off. He grew frustrated when the new one ran continuously as well, and called a plumber friend. He had to face the geographical facts of life in dealing with a filled-in tideflat; that he basically had his finger in a huge dike. "He said, 'You're trying to pump Puget Sound from your building.' "

John Bennett

The entrance to the new Silver Cloud Hotel.

Stadium Silver Cloud opened on 1046 1st Avenue South, across the street from Safeco Field.

From one side of SoDo to the other, and it apparently doesn't matter how close a company is located to the waterfront, the sump pump is a necessary piece of equipment for doing business. Just ask John Bennett or Gary Eastes.

Bennett used to occupy and own the building at 1501 1st Avenue South, currently catering to the heavy-metal nightclub Motor. He sold

antique jukeboxes. While dealing with an always-damp ground floor, he bought a new sump pump to replace an old one that wouldn't shut off. He grew frustrated when the new one ran continuously as well, and called a plumber friend. He had to face the geographical facts of life in dealing with a filled-in tideflat; that he basically had his finger in a huge dike.

"He said, 'You're trying to pump Puget Sound from your building,' " Bennett recalled with a laugh.

Eastes family members own

the building at 923 South Bay View Street, which houses several tenants and sits across the way from their Lee and Eastes Tank Lines facility on Airport Way South. Sump pumps are running around the clock in the basement of what is called the Bayview Building. Turn them off, and there's an immediate six feet of water collected inside. Seashells have been uncovered here. This is tideflat, often fresh tideflat, that won't go away.

"If we have another bad earthquake, Airport Way will fall in and all the rest of the buildings will disappear," said Gary Eastes, whose nearby truck shop is built on pilings. "That building will still be here."

Look What We Found

Turning over fill on a 6th Avenue South job site in SoDo, construction workers uncovered huge amounts of charred debris. As these men dug six feet down in an area 80 feet long that would later hold a new warehouse, they excavated blackened wood, plates, bottles and other trinkets. They pulled up newspapers with classified ads that were still readable. It was determined that this had been one of the dumping grounds for the 1889 Seattle fire, a blaze that leveled most of the waterfront with a fury. Stuff was tossed in this once marshy area as the central downtown region was rebuilt.

"I'm sure people took home great stuff," said Bill Oseran, Seattle Textile owner and SoDo land developer who was privy to the discovery.

On the other side of SoDo, archeologists were positioned on-site, poised to inspect any artifacts uncovered, while contractors, preparing to lay a foundation for a Starbucks-owned, seven-story building with a 2010 completion date, tore up a parking lot on 1st Avenue South. A huge pile of decomposed lumber was pulled out and inspected. The overturned lot, located next door to the historic Triangle Pub, had housed a turn-of-the-century sawmill, horse and saddle shop and service station before all the buildings were razed.

Workers were amazed at the 10- to 15-foot layer of wood that was discovered down at the 35-foot level, especially with the water table at a bare nine feet. The stuff could have been 80 or 90 years old. Two gas tanks also were dug up and removed. It was no big deal to the archeologists, who sat perched like a squadron of building inspectors but were hoping to find something of more value and historic relevance. The hardhat workers, however, were impressed with their glimpse of an old and long-buried Seattle.

"It was identifiable because it was all cut, one by fours for example," said Darin Dougherty, assistant superintendent for the Lease Crutcher Lewis construction company. "There was a wealth of lumber dug out of the site. It was all wood millings. It was in a bay or they stacked it. It was really something."

It was old SoDo meeting new SoDo.

Henry Liebman and Dave Gering both work out of bland, well-worn office buildings located about a mile apart in Seattle's sprawling industrial area. The similarities end there. With great conviction, each man has tried to mold the SoDo District into something that couldn't be more different in concept and more roundly debated than if the Democratic and Republican parties had dreamed up this stuff.

Liebman, SoDo's largest private land owner with 54 acres of holdings, wants to provide a business facelift to this well-utilized corridor and improve its appearance. Gering says SoDo looks just fine the way it is, insisting that any further cosmetic

Henry Liebman

change to the workingman's neighborhood would leave it with something that resembles a gated community, with his industry constituents left on the outside. Liebman and his American Life real estate company have elaborate plans to bring sleek and airy business space to SoDo in the form of five- to seven-story buildings, creating corporate campuses close to the downtown core of Seattle. Gering and his Georgetown-based Manufacturing and Industrial

Council of Seattle have made it their mission to maintain welding shops and warehouses in their perspiring and aging state, preserving a blue-collar area he says was meant to be different from its uptown neighbors.

"There is an industrial place, but it's not here," Liebman said. "It's West Marginal Way to South Park. That's where industrial is. That's where Gering's members are."

Gering's counter-argument: "This is still an industrial area. People were trying to get it rezoned 10 years ago and said industry is dead. Instead, industry has grown."

> *"There is an industrial place, but it's not here. It's West Marginal Way to South Park. That's where industrial is. That's where Gering's members are."*
>
> Henry Liebman

SoDo's Yin & Yang

The amazing thing about these two people is they hardly resemble the ogres that the opposing sides portray them to be, claims based solely on their stated beliefs over what to do with this unsophisticated southern section of the city. Liebman, an immigration attorney turned creative land developer, is a slender man with an easy manner that belies his aggressiveness in patching together business deals. Gering, a former newspaper reporter turned persuasive heavy-industry lobbyist, is a bigger and louder person, relentless in delivering his message yet polite in manner and often apologetic about his bluntness.

What's not in dispute is SoDo's prime location in the city. It borders Seattle's high-rise district on one side and the waterfront on another, making it a highly coveted piece of real estate. For now,

Gering has the necessary political muscle on his side, with Mayor Greg Nickels introducing zoning legislation in 2008 that made it more difficult to diversify business pursuits and erect the bigger buildings that Liebman favors. Not by coincidence, the restrictions came about after Liebman had used his vast knowledge of immigration law to secure foreign investment in exchange for his partners receiving permanent American resident status and a healthy financial return.

At one point in 2009, Liebman claimed ownership of 26 SoDo properties that collectively cost $242 million to obtain and renovate. General market conditions and demand caused an increase in rents and land prices that created neighborhood friction from those directly affected and led to the aforementioned political intervention. Labor groups and others complained that their blue-collar jobs were being swallowed up by one man's hard-line real-estate dealings. Seattle's mayor shared similar concerns. Nickels acted quickly to introduce SoDo zoning changes that limited building height, floor space and office usage, partially in response to Liebman's rapid-fire land purchases. At least that's how Liebman viewed it.

"The unions were (angry) at Nickels, because he had made too many deals with developers," Liebman said. "He used us as a whipping boy." To which Gering responded, "If we didn't do something to stop that, it would have taken everything away. The person profiting would be richer for it, but the rest of us wouldn't."

Still the Same after All these Years

Behind this never-ending tug of war, SoDo remains a daily bustle of trucks intersecting with freight trains and light-rail cars on three separate lines that repeatedly

2006 aerial view of SoDo during a workday.

back up traffic between 1st Avenue South and 4th Avenue South in mid-day. There are blocks of unpaved roads full of craters and paved roads full of severe dips and potholes, and sizable sections of torn-up roadway, some of it facilitating waterfront tunnel construction and some of it leading to freeway expansion. There is Liebman's mass remodeling effort involving buildings in the middle of 1st Avenue South, turning worn-out 1910 stuff into glistening 2010 upgrades. There are roughly a half-dozen nightclubs on the same street livening up

the neighborhood at night, including Showbox Sodo, Motor and Seven that promote their shows while others do business without signage or any evidence that they exist except for the rumble of evening sounds. There is more than one building lost to fire damage, either under repair or sitting idle in a neglectful state. In the middle of SoDo there is a three-barn recycling center, complete with roaring trucks, circling seagulls and flying debris, contributing to a busy, messy place.

Diversity Reigns

Cobalt, an online auto parts company, works in the same SoDo block as Outdoor Research, an outfit that makes military clothing. On one end of the neighborhood Rosanna Imports sells custom tableware while on the other J.D. Ott Company produces aerospace parts. Seattle's original Krispy Kreme outlet keeps everyone in donuts

SoDo is getting more and more gentrified; here's a view of the new BMW dealership on 6th Avenue South.

and coffee, while a few blocks away Washington Chain and Supply is responsible for outfitting ships in anchors. Ecohaus, a green-oriented building-supply company, operates near Charlie's Produce, a place that stuffs greens and other salad fixings into bags. Macrina and Gai's bakeries prepare food, while Elo's Philly Grill and Mr. D's Greek Restaurant and Bar serve it.

SoDo has also been forced to make room for countless government-related outlets. Among them are the Metro bus yard, Seattle City Light power station, King County Metro garage and bus yard, U.S. Postal Service's garage, Evergreen Treatment Services, a state sex-offender halfway house, Seattle Public Utilities offices and Sound Transit's railyard. There's also a sizeable law-enforcement presence, with the Seattle police guild office, Seattle police training center, Seattle police evidence storage warehouse and state toxicology lab. There are Coast Guard offices and piers, federal warehouses, the state Liquor Board and John Stanford Center for Educational Excellence. There is no shortage of union representation, with the neighborhood offering a labor hall for hospital workers,

> *"There's an old saying that if you get in the way of progress you get run over."*
>
> Tom McQuaid

janitors and others, another for grocery, retail and service-sector jobs, and yet another for longshoremen and warehousemen.

Mostly, among this clearly diverse collection of tenants, there are mixed opinions about what SoDo ultimately should be. "We've got Oz up here and the city says we're going to keep it as a cornfield," said SoDo realtor Rick Osterhout, a senior vice president for GVA Kidder Mathews.

"I'm a contrarian," said Bill Rosen, Alaskan Copper Works president, giving a different viewpoint. "A city should have an area that looks like downtown Beirut."

Shifting with the Economic Times – A SoDo Tradition

From sawmills and shipyards in SoDo's earliest days, the neighborhood experienced a big shift to machine shops, steel mills and meat-packing plants. Warehouses were introduced on a large scale once the Port of Seattle reclaimed the waterfront following World War II, and decreased once the bulk of container shipping abruptly went from railcars to the trucking industry. And after tenants fled to the suburbs, needing bigger and cheaper facilities to make and store things, SoDo opened a wide berth for home-improvement retailers and people selling cabinets, granite countertops, lighting and flooring. With each passing decade the industrial presence in SoDo has moved farther south, initially giving way to the professional sports stadiums, with Safeco Field replacing the outdated Kingdome across

the street and Qwest Field occupying the site of the dismantled dome. Many of the surviving fabricating shops are huddled around South Spokane Street.

"It would be a real travesty to see the city lose this manufacturing and industrial space," SoDo artist and landowner David Hutchthausen said. "Industry used to go to Jackson Street (in Pioneer Square), and then it was pushed to Royal Brougham, and then it was pushed to Atlantic, and now they want to push it to Holgate. They're nibbling at the edge."

> *"Is a business like Starbucks incompatible to what goes on here? Hell no. Putting artificial zoning on things isn't going to keep people from wanting to build here. The market is the market. It's going to be what it's going to be."*
>
> Bill Oseran

Siren Tavern

Someone else's misfortune was once everyone's good luck at the Siren Tavern.

Throughout the 1960s and into the next decade, the SoDo District drinking establishment, located across the street from Fire Station 14 on 4th Avenue South, used to offer a round of drinks on the house or a round of discounted beers to customers whenever a siren went off in the neighborhood and firefighters were called to an incident.

That practice ended abruptly when tavern customers repeatedly made bogus calls to the station and other firefighters pestered their peers to flip on a siren, just to get a bargain serving. The late Helen Strotz, who ran the tavern with her husband, Andy, cut everyone off when things got out of hand.

"I started working here in 1989 and it was no longer legal or prudent to do that by then," said Connie Longrie, Siren Tavern's current owner and originally a bartender. "They had firefighters calling up their buddies to set off the alarms. It's a piece of history now."

Located at 3403 4th Avenue South and tucked into a mall setting, the Siren Tavern remains a popular place for the SoDo working men and women. Thursday and Friday nights draw big crowds to a place that opened in 1963.

The Siren Tavern is one of SoDo's most popular drinking establishments.

The Western Steel Casting Crew circa 1970s.

Firefighter memorabilia once filled the walls until a past owner sold it without permission. Steel workers used to flock to the place after their shifts before the mills went out of business. A crew from Western Steel Casting (see accompanying photo) once hopped on a forklift and drove it to the tavern, running out of propane fuel after they arrived, leaving them scrambling to figure out how to get the rig back to the plant. Truckers and other union workers still can be found seated at the bar after workdays are over.

"This always was the heart of Seattle, blue collar," said Danny Muncy, a tavern regular who has worked as a machinist and truck driver. "Come in here with a tie on, and you were either a cop or a salesman and had about 10 minutes to get that tie off."

While labor leaders attempt to preserve as much industrial space as possible, developers say anything north of South Spokane Street should be fair game for urban renewal. Others say anything in SoDo west of the doomed Alaskan Way Viaduct should be preserved for industry, while anything goes to the east. Still others maintain that the railroad tracks between 2nd Avenue South and 3rd Avenue South should be the demarcation line, with industry hugging the west side and business diversity filling the east end.

The SoDo of the Future

Developer Greg Smith envisions a section of SoDo becoming one of Seattle's more progressive links to a future way of doing business. He has unveiled plans to create a "green" auto row along 6th Avenue South, not far from where a newly built BMW dealership has a foothold, or possibly on Airport Way South, or both. He has met with alternative-energy automakers in Silicon Valley. He has welcomed gas-saving electric bikes, motorcycles and Segway scooters to join in this environment.

"It's such an opportunity

> *"We're a progressive city, a 'green city,' and we should be leading the charge. We're really the only place in the city that could do it. You can create tax revenue and it is win, win, win. We have engineers here who have built the Dreamliner, the most fuel-efficient jet, and Paccar, which builds fuel-efficient trucks. We have the brainpower here and we have the opportunity to create new industry in Seattle. We could provide jobs for people with engineering degrees and people who didn't graduate from college."*
>
> Greg Smith

because of the collapse of Detroit and the emphasis of the Obama administration to pursue technologies that are not oil-independent," Smith said. "We're a progressive city, a 'green city,' and we should be leading the charge. We're really the only place in the city that could do it. You can create tax revenue and it is win, win, win. We have engineers here who have built the Dreamliner, the most fuel-efficient jet, and Paccar, which builds fuel-efficient trucks. We have the brainpower here and we have the opportunity to create new industry in Seattle. We could provide jobs for people with engineering degrees and people who didn't graduate from college."

Ironically, Smith is determined to establish his "green" district not far from where SoDo once housed a strip of red-light brothels long phased out of business, including a long-closed diesel service station on Airport Way South that allegedly employed a cashier who

> *"You have to think five, 10, 15 years down the line. Because of the container property, you're not going to have housing. We have to make what we have here work better. I respect Dave Gering and people who want industrial here, but we have to get beyond that and combine the two sides."*
>
> Mike Peringer

doubled as an opportunistic prostitute. Regardless of the color scheme, most everyone agrees there will be greater pressure in the future to either eliminate industry in SoDo altogether or greatly reduce it in favor of alternative offerings.

The Old SoDo Folks Weigh In

"There's Allentown to the north, that's what I call it, and the only place you can go now with growth is

K2 is one of the nation's leading manufacturers of Nordic equipment and accessories.

"This is where we should have modern industry. A lot of companies want to be downtown. This is where we should have modern industry, but they've made it difficult to build something new."

Henry Liebman

south," said SoDo businessman Dave Ederer, referring to Paul Allen's ambitious development of the formerly industrial-minded South Lake Union locality. "SoDo will be residential some day. The economics will drive it. The eclectic nature of the area might be fun."

"I don't think there will ever be a consensus on it," said Gary Stratiner, who moved his Puget Sound Pipe Company to Kent, and now has business locations inside and outside of SoDo. "There will always be opposition to local industry. It's going to happen. There's only so much land. Where are you going to go?"

"There's an old saying that if you get in the way of progress you get run over," said Tom McQuaid, owner of Nordic Cold Storage at 547 Occidental Avenue South, rather pointedly.

Some developers envision office space running down 6th Avenue South and retail filling up most of 1st Avenue South. Fourth Avenue South already is a mix of both. In some cases, exceptions have been made to the strict zoning guidelines. Real-estate broker Art Wahl helped facilitate the move of ski-maker K2 Sports from Vashon Island to a new home at 4201 6th Avenue South. The company wasn't heavy industry, and it took some serious lobbying to sign off on its SoDo aspirations.

Mike Peringer stands in front of an ArtWorks mural.

But in the end the city wasn't going to turn away an upwardly mobile company with 200 workers.

"This is an evolution and the change in our commerce," Wahl said. "You find usage living closer to the city. Unless I'm crazy, over time this will be a retail treasure. Manufacturing jobs will disappear. They will tell you it's not true. And this isn't South Lake Union. This is less expensive. It's housing for the middle class vs. high-end condos elsewhere. This area has a lot of potential."

While Florida-raised Liebman, a University of Washington alumnus, is the noted exception, a majority of the largest and most influential SoDo landowners are old Seattle. They're from families that grew up together, went to school together and now own much of SoDo together, and collectively they're very reluctant to part with it, mulling far greater returns down the line. The Stratiners, Amicks, Ederers, Stacks and Soules all went to Roosevelt High School. The Rabels, Shermans, Frinks and Oserans attended Garfield. The Rosens graduated from Ballard, the Leavitts were Franklin products and the Cochranes received their education from Queen Anne. They're city-raised and well-acquainted in many respects. "Dave Ederer dated a Stack sister," Robb Stack pointed out. "There's familiarity there."

Let Us Make the Decision

While nearly all of these families have operated some form of heavy industry, and some still do, nearly all of them have held on to their

Two of Seattle's city councilmen, Bruce Harrell and Richard Conlin, are among many officials evaluating the future of SoDo.

SoDo properties and the notion that they should be able to do something creative,

"At the end of the day, it's still a balancing act. I don't see it changing its definition in the near future. I also don't support a blanket prohibition over utilizing properties. I definitely want a diversity of occupations."

Bruce Harrell

if not non-industrial, with their land if they choose.

"Most people don't work with their hands anymore," said Bill Oseran, Seattle Textile Company owner and SoDo real-estate developer. "There is no fish-processing for the waterfront anymore. It has evolved into the aquarium and restaurants and tour boats. The space has to get used by somebody and should go to the best and highest use, knowing it has to

be somewhat compatible to the waterfront and railroad. Is a business like Starbucks incompatible to what goes on here? Hell no. Putting artificial zoning on things isn't going to keep people from wanting to build here. The market is the market. It's going to be what it's going to be."

Doug Glant, president of Pacific Iron and Metal, still operates a "heavy" industry, running a scrap-metal company in the shadows of the city's skyscrapers that has existed at the same address for eight decades. Yet Glant strongly believes he has the right to do whatever he wants with the family property. He made that clear when Nickels called him, seeking Glant's support in the mayor's re-election campaign. Glant informed the incumbent rather pointedly that he was no fan of the aggressive SoDo zoning regulations, and there would be political ramifications because of them.

Andy's Diner

Andy's Diner was one SoDo freight train that everyone wanted to hop. For more than a half-century this collection of seven railcars pieced together at 2963 4th Avenue South supplied Boeing executives at the highest level and working-class people alike with a wildly popular place to eat, providing they could tolerate waiting in the often hour-long lunch line that stretched out the front door.

Clients were hosted. Business deals were closed. Appetites were well-sated.

"It was Rainier Club south," said SoDo businessman Dave Ederer, comparing it to Seattle's most exclusive private club.

Two men originally from Pennsylvania and named Andy ran the restaurant from 1949 to 1991. Andy Nagy opened it, and Andy

Andy Yurkanin never forgot the name of a customer.

Yurkanin, Nagy's nephew, gave it personality. "Little Andy" actually was a much bigger man than his uncle. They were 50-50 owners, working side by side for 25 years.

Nagy opened the diner inside one railcar. Over a six-year period, others were purchased from a local junkyard and from Seattle City Light's Skagit dam-building project. The most visible car, one of President Franklin D. Roosevelt's campaign transporters, was picked up at auction in Minnesota.

The two Andys purchased FDR's railcar for $18,000, and then spent

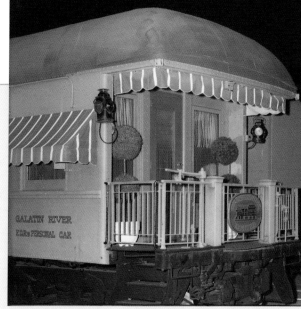

The back end of FDR's rail car at Andy's Diner.

$75,000 on the remodel, rewiring it, putting in bigger doors and doing whatever was necessary to bring it up to building code.

"I still have the headboards where Eleanor Roosevelt slept here and FDR slept here," Yurkanin said.

The railcar theme and good food and service made Andy's Diner an instant hit in an area that didn't offer many dining options. The most popular item was a skirt steak, marinated in barbecue sauce and tossed on the broiler. Eight hundred to 1,000 pounds of beef would be consumed daily.

"We called it the 'Slippery Steak,' " said Phil MacFadden of SoDo's Puget Sound Industries.

"It outsold everything on the menu," Yurkanin confirmed.

Andy's Diner was such a busy place at the noon hour that 700 to a thousand people would show up for lunch every day. One woman working the 11-seat counter might serve 100 people in a half-hour. Chef Larry Asaba could remember 100 orders at a time without writing them down.

People could eat in the Club Car, the Round House Room, the Sidetrack Room, the Executive Car or the Caboose Room. Martini lunches were frequent. A Derailer was an alcoholic beverage served by the diner in a bucket with two straws.

"I used to take clients there for lunch and dinners," said Rex Holt, former Peat Belting owner. "I'd have suppliers come in from Japan, and it was good food, and they liked sitting in the railcars and reading the history."

(continued on page 126)

"I said, 'Greg, I won't support you, I won't give you a dime, because you've cost me millions,' " Glant said, who envisions a much different industrial district some day. "SoDo will be thriving, but it won't be industrial area. My land has a good future. SoDo has a good future. I'm bullish on SoDo, very bearish on SoDo industry."

Yet another voice belongs to SoDo land owner and developer Tom Leavitt, usually a labor backer, just not when it comes to this neighborhood. "I'm a very strong supporter of unions, but in this case they're just dead wrong," Leavitt said. "The idea of restraining development down here is wrong. They're shooting themselves in the foot. The development of that area will come very slowly. This blind denial of reality is so counterproductive for the city and everybody."

Touting a Merger of the Minds

Mike Peringer, SoDo Business Association president and marketing director for Process Heating Company, has touted a merger of the minds in proposing a business model for the future. "Nobody is looking behind the end of their nose," Peringer said. "You have to think five, 10, 15 years down the line. Because of the container property, you're not going to have housing. We have to make what we have here work better. I respect Dave Gering and people who want industrial here, but we have to get beyond that and combine the two sides."

At Alaskan Copper Works, Doug and Bill Rosen are among the siblings who run the family empire, but they don't always see things the same way. They're a dozen years apart in age. As Bill Rosen points out, he was raised during the Eisenhower era and his younger sibling was brought up during the

Age of Aquarius. One is more old-school conformist, the other a vocal and persistent protester. SoDo's zoning laws arouse different reactions from them. Bill Rosen, chairman and chief executive officer, calls himself the foreman of the ranch. That leaves the blunt Doug Rosen, Alaskan Copper Works vice president, as a modern-day land speculator hardly set on old ways of doing business.

"The labor unions are critical of any development south of town," Doug Rosen said. "The Port of Seattle management is stuck in the sway of the labor unions. We have a terrible political problem. Over time, (development) will naturally happen. Or you'll get left with a lot of vacant lots."

A Numbers Conflict

Gering says he has tried to preserve upwards of 60,000 industrial jobs interspersed throughout SoDo. Doug Rosen of Alaskan Copper and Brass says there are no more than

30,000 that qualify as true industrial, that the numbers have been greatly inflated to protect labor interests, and that the city doesn't have a ready definition of what qualifies as industrial employment. Liebman says there aren't even 60,000 people in SoDo and to the extent traditional industrial workers exist they are mostly south of Spokane Street along the Duwamish River. Little wonder that Gering, when speaking of his chief adversary in preserving SoDo's industrial zoning interests, does not necessarily list Liebman as public enemy No. 1. He reserves that spot for someone he feels should be more of an industrial protectionist rather than an industrial protagonist at heart.

"The upside of this is Henry is better than the Rosens," the MIC director said. "Doug will make it sound like they want big-box retail."

To which Doug Rosen responded, "Seattle has

(continued from page 124)

"Andy's Diner was the place to do business," said Frank Firmani, construction company owner and real estate developer.

Yurkanin used to stand up front and greet his customers, most of them by name, with his personalized service another reason people clamored to the diner.

"This one guy, Orville, moved to Huntsville, Ala., to work for Boeing, and he was away for five years," Yurkanin recalled. "He came back and bet his friend that Andy would remember him. They were standing in line and I said, 'Hey Orville, when did you get back in town?' The other guy lost the bet and had to buy lunch. I was very good about remembering people and remembering names."

Sadly, the landmark diner went from two Andys in charge to just one when Nagy died in 1980. He had just finished playing handball at the Washington Athletic Club when he shook hands with his opponent and collapsed. Nagy was 60.

Yurkanin stayed on for another 11 years before retiring. His son, T.J., ran the place for nearly five years before three men, none of them named Andy, bought it. In the change-over, the eatery lost a lot of luster, closed for a few months and was reopened in 2008 as a Chinese restaurant with a new name, the Orient Express. There was no opposition to the name from the old guard.

"I suggested they call it Orient Express," Yurkanin said. "It didn't make me sad. You're going to have changes in life."

The green FDR railcar remains prominently displayed outside, with the following words painted across it: "Assuming the presidency at the depth of the Great Depression, FDR helped the American people regain faith in themselves." A cat bunks underneath it, presumably to keep the rats away.

Yurkanin stops by for lunch on occasion. He likes to reminisce. The owners always greet him and treat him well. He offers advice to them when asked.

"I loved to come to work," Yurkanin said. "I didn't know who I was going to meet that day. You could be a guy who was a millionaire or a guy who had overalls on. That was the nice thing about it."

The interior of the original Andy's Diner.

The original Andy's Diner morphed into the Orient Express in 2008.

to be more like San Francisco. All it has to be is an urban marketplace. Nice place to live. Good food. Part transportation needs. Let industry go where it goes. In San Francisco, it went to Sacramento, or it's on the way to Sacramento. They're not trying to go to Sacramento here."

Gering better hope that Doug Rosen, if not Henry Liebman, remains the worst of his problems. Developer Greg Smith has pondered taking highly creative steps to change the city's stance on residential and retail development in SoDo and elsewhere in the city. His great, great grandfather, Leonard P. Smith, was Seattle's mayor in 1880-1881. Could City Hall handle another Smith at the top rung of leadership?

A Political Slant

"I've thought about running for mayor," the modern-day Smith acknowledged. "I find many politicians are afraid to be progressive. They stay really close to the tree and try not to do things that are progressive. And when they miss, they get voted out of office."

Seattle city councilmen Bruce Harrell and Richard Conlin are among those entrusted with pointing SoDo in a future direction. These politicians and their peers have been inundated with studies, statistics, boundaries and philosophies over what to do next with this hot-button subject. Adding to the confusion is the fact that one plot of SoDo land might have manufacturing in the back, located next to a warehouse used to store goods, while retail is selling its wares out front. So how does this property get classified? Is it industrial or commercial? Inventories only serve to muddle the issues, not settle them. Meantime, the only safe position for these policy-makers to take is middle ground.

"I think because of Seattle's unique history, in our lifetimes and the lifetimes of my children, it will still maintain mostly manufacturing, industrial and maritime use, but will still see some smart pockets of retail growth," Harrell said. "At the end of the day, it's still a balancing act. I don't see it changing its definition in the near future. I also don't support a blanket prohibition over utilizing properties. I definitely want a diversity of occupations."

Conlin said previous SoDo zoning restrictions are too vague, maybe even outdated, and haven't won him over. He wants better definitions for industrial offerings before agreeing to hard and fast boundaries.

"I don't think it was necessarily drawn with a complete understanding of where we're going in the future," he said. "It's important to preserve industrial, but we're going to struggle until we figure out where we want industrial to be."

We're Fine Just the Way We Are

One business that likes things just the way they are in the SoDo District is M. Bloch Company. This huge scrap yard at the southern tip of the area has trucks whizzing in and out filled with big loads of metal. Inside the gates, there are sturdy cranes in constant motion depositing big chunks of the recycled stuff in metal containers. There is a lot of interconnected heavy-industry activity going on at all times. Those who run this yard were more than a little surprised when Terminal 108 across the street was converted into a string of home-improvement retail outlets. The bustling scrap trucks and the new-found customer traffic aren't a compatible mix on Colorado Avenue South that separates these businesses.

"This wasn't supposed to happen and we were disappointed when it did," M. Bloch president Joel

Richards said. "The mayor said he wanted to keep industrial as industrial."

Or as Steve Crary, the outspoken counterman at Blanchard Auto Electric Company at 640 South Spokane Street and another of those resistant to widespread neighborhood change, put it: "SoDo should secede from the state. We just want our SoDo."

A Barrier to Progress

That leaves Liebman and Gering as major opposing forces to duke it out over what's best for SoDo. The controversial real-estate

"There is an industrial place, but it's not here. It's the Henry Liebmans and Dave Gerings of the world aren't that far apart. The city needs to say, 'You're right and you're right, and there needs to be something in between.' "

Mike Peringer

developer likely will wait out the opposition while building his empire. He's been seeking property elsewhere in the city, if not throughout the Puget Sound region, and he easily could determine that better commercial development opportunity awaits him outside of Seattle's industrial war zone.

"They're working real hard at chasing the capital out of the area," Liebman said. "I might have to go somewhere else. Tacoma and Everett need all the help they can get and they don't have these restrictions. If zoning makes development impossible, capital and the developers will leave the area. And it's not just me. It's other people, too."

While Liebman impatiently mulls his SoDo investment options, Gering was asked to identify the best examples of area industrial companies that are prospering. He named Manson Construction Company, which has offered

six-figure employee salaries and was responsible for rebuilding the collapsed I-35 bridge in Minneapolis 100 days ahead of schedule. He named B&G Machining, which was described as never busier in building diesel engines, to the point of opening a second plant. And he pointed to Nucor Steel, operating one of the more profitable steel-production plants in the country.

There was just one thing wrong with this big picture: None of these businesses are located in SoDo. They have either Georgetown or West Seattle addresses. Who's bluffing whom when it comes to preserving or deserting SoDo? Gering or Liebman?

"What if I brought Microsoft here?" challenged Liebman, noting that industrial jobs need to be better defined. "Would you keep them out?"

Volleyed back Gering, "I've talked to Henry and I'm not saying he's evil. He's a very bright guy. But he used that

(immigration) program to make money."

And Back & Forth it Goes

Liebman has suggested that a sudden slew of vacant SoDo buildings could force the removal of the city-zoning limits. Unfazed, Gering mentioned there are 230 Boeing suppliers located in Seattle that will always need a place to do business, and supposed vacancies represent an unfounded threat. Liebman counters the property is too valuable to hold back from diverse business interests, especially since SoDo provides an epicenter for the Puget Sound transportation grid, with Interstates 5 and 90, State Route 99, old rail and the new light-rail all intersecting within blocks of each other not far from the harbor's edge. Gering wanted to know that if the zoning gloves eventually came off, who would control SoDo traffic and keep the Port of Seattle from getting overwhelmed by the expected logjam of vehicles?

"This is where we should have modern industry," Liebman insisted. "A lot of companies want to be downtown."

Giving in a little to office and retail, Gering allowed, "I would say 1st and 4th Avenues are where you might see gentrification; I can't deny it. But it's surprising how many industrial companies are still there."

Finally, Some Agreement

One principle in which these men share agreement is that SoDo probably isn't the best place for residential buildings, outside of the few artist lofts and north-end condominiums already in place. Liebman, contrary to widespread belief, isn't interested in bringing housing options to SoDo for two reasons: 1) the land is flat, leaving few water views to sell; and 2) the land is far too contaminated to clean up to

Would a cataclysmic earthquake return SoDo to this scene: a view of Seattle's waterfront from Beacon Hill, circa 1881?

meet residential building codes without absorbing exorbitant costs. There's no telling what sort of hazardous waste lies beneath this industrial area. The Burger King restaurant near Liebman's office previously was a battery shop and the soil on that site is said to be saturated with battery acid, which means Liebman's headquarters likely sits over the toxic goo, too.

Liebman prefers to build new five- to seven-story midrises. He recently put one up on South Utah Street and has others in the planning stages across the street, able to pull off this development because

the properties are bigger and have more lenient zoning restrictions. However, most SoDo properties encompass 10,000 square feet or smaller, which usually limits a developer to putting up just two floors.

"This is where we should have modern industry, but they've made it difficult to build something new," Liebman said. "Zoning has to allow us a little more retail to service these buildings. You should be able to rent the top floor to office. This is the prototype. That's where I see the future here. This product exists everywhere else in the

world. People are going to look for close-in locations. You could have modern buildings here. Those things would rock."

The Gering rebuttal: "You have to step back and say what's good for the community: The value of industry or someone making huge amounts of money?"

So Here We Are Today, Not Much Different than a Century Ago

In the near future, Liebman could have his way and totally change the look of SoDo with newer and bigger buildings.

Or Gering's determined efforts on behalf of the local welders and coppersmiths will keep the area in exactly the same shape for an extended time.

"The Henry Liebmans and Dave Gerings of the world aren't that far apart," Peringer said. "The city needs to say, 'You're right and you're right, and there needs to be something in between.' "

Yet there is a third and far less desirable option for SoDo that could make everyone's differences moot, that only a made-for-TV script could love, that hopefully is no more than a fictional afterthought.

"Long term, I don't know what's going to happen here," admitted Gering. "There's not a tree down there to hug. This is the worst earthquake area in the city. It's a huge earthquake area. With the seismic risk, this all goes first."

The labor leader made that wisecrack only to put a light-hearted spin around a hot-button question. Yet consider what could happen if the "Big One" hits the Puget Sound region. SoDo's unstable soil might rapidly crumble and liquefy.

Below the century-old surface, all those underground saltwater rivers that already lead from Puget Sound to the Pacific Coast Feather Company and other indiscriminate industrial-area businesses might turn into rapidly swelling lakes and ponds that no amount of sump pumps could handle.

If the unthinkable took place, with developers and heavy industrial frantically pulling on life preservers and scrambling into rowboats, SoDo would be tideland once again.

Special Thanks

Many thanks from the author and publisher to the following people who greatly helped in the creation of this book.

Jeffrey Long, Pacific Coast Feather Company

Paul Dorpat

Bill Rabel, Star Rentals

Dave Ederer, Ederer Cranes

Mick McCoy, O.B. Williams

Rex Holt

Blaine Dempke and Robert LeCoque, Markey Machinery

Joel Richards, M. Bloch Company

Bill & Doug Rosen, Alaskan Copper Works

Hal Amick, Amick Metal

Doug Glant, Pacific Iron and Metal

Al Aurilio

Henry Castle

Tom "Tully" O'Keefe

Harold & Robb Stack, Stack Steel

Ernie Sherman, Sherman Supply

Warren, John & Kevin Cochrane, Millwork Supply

Gary & Bruce Eastes, Lee and Eastes

Stewart & Scott Soules, System Transfer and Storage

Art Mendelsohn

Dave Eskenazi

MOHAI

University of Washington Press

Nicolette Bromberg, Visual Materials Curator at UW, & Her Staff

Margene Ridout

Bill Leiendecker

Andy Yurkanin

Del Bates

Charlie Sheldon, Port of Seattle

Frank Firmani

Jack Block Sr.

Tom McQuaid

Bruce Harrell, Seattle City Council

Greg Smith

David Freiboth

Gary Stratiner, Puget Sound Pipe and Supply Company

Henry Liebman

Steve Loeb, Alaska Distributors

Gary Volchok, C.B. Richard Ellis

Jim White, Mobile Crane

Neil Skogland, Ederer Crane

Peter Miller

Eric Scigliano

Frank Stagen, Kevin Daniels & Kristia Cannon, Nitze-Stagen

Steve Cunetta & Jim Copacino, Copacino+Fujikado

Chuck LeFevre, Esquin Wine

Mike Peringer

Johnny O'Brien

Steve Kidd

Ben VanHouten

Corky Trewin

Seattle Seahawks

Julie Kerssen, Seattle Municipal Archives

Bill Oseran, Seattle Textile

Eric Blank

Tim Demmon

James Dillon

Scott Andrews

Dave Rost, McKinstry Company

Debra & Ron Wise, Pecos Pit

Bev Akada, Costco

Dave Gering

Richard Conlin, Seattle City Council

Rick Osterhout, GVA Kidder Mathews

Connie Longrie, Siren Tavern

Photo Credits*

Cover, pages 1 & 2: From "History of Seattle - Volume 1," by Clarence B. Bagley, S.J. Clarke Publishing Company, 1916

Page 4 (Yesler): From "History of Seattle - Volume 2," by Clarence B. Bagley, S.J. Clarke Publishing Company, 1916

Page 4 (Semple): From "A History of the Puget Sound Country - Its Resources, Its Commerce and Its People," by Col. William Farrand Prosser, Lewis Publishing Company, 1903

Page 5: From "History of Seattle - Volume 1," by Clarence B. Bagley, S.J. Clarke Publishing Company, 1916

Pages 9 & 15: Courtesy of Peat Belting.

Page 10: Courtesy of Star Rentals

Page 13: Portrait by John Taliaferro; courtesy of Ederer LLC

Page 14: Courtesy of O.B. Williams

Page 16: Courtesy of Markey Machinery Company

Page 17: Courtesy of Bloch Steel Industries

Pages 18 (Al Aurilio), 21 & 22: Courtesy of Pacific Iron and Metal

Page 18: Courtesy of Henry Castle

Pages 23 & 25: From "History of Seattle - Volume 2," by Clarence B. Bagley, S.J. Clarke Publishing Company, 1916

Page 27: Courtesy of Millwork Supply

Page 30: Courtesy of Sherman Supply Company

Page 31: Courtesy of Lee & Eastes Tank Lines

Pages 35 & 37: PEMCO Webster & Stevens Collection, MOHAI (1986.10.10788)

Page 36: Courtesy of Art Mendelsohn

Page 38: Seattle Post-Intelligencer Collection, MOHAI (1986.5.3610.2)

Page 39: Courtesy of Dave Eskenazi

Page 40: Courtesy of University of Washington Press

Page 41: Courtesy of University of Washington Press

Page 42: Photos courtesy of Bill Oseran

Page 44: Courtesy of Leiendecker Family

Page 48: Courtesy of David Eskenazi

Page 49: Official U.S. Government photo courtesy of Dr. J David Rogers of the Missouri University of Science and Technology

Page 51: Courtesy of University of Washington Libraries, Special Collections, A. Curtis 1653

Page 52: Seattle Post-Intelligencer Collection, MOHAI (PI26323)

Page 57: Courtesy of Nitze-Stagen & Co.

Page 58: Courtesy of www.warchat.org

Pages 61 & 64: Courtesy of Ederer LLC

Page 62: Courtesy of Gary Stratiner

Page 66: Courtesy of www.bcuniversal.com

Page 67: Courtesy of Peter Miller Books

Page 74: Courtesy of Nitze-Stagen & Company

Page 75: Courtesy of Copacino+Fujikado

Pages 76 & 77: Courtesy of Mike Perringer

Page 81: Courtesy of Chuck LeFevre

Pages 83 & 85: Courtesy of Seattle Municipal Archives (from Document 7216)

Page 84: Courtesy of Corky Trewin and the Seattle Seahawks

Page 86: Courtesy of Steve Kidd

Pages 86 & 87: Courtesy of Dave Eskenazi

Page 87: Courtesy of MOHAI (SHS5595)

Page 89: Courtesy of Ben VanHouten

Page 93: Courtesy of Nitze-Stagen

Page 98: Courtesy of James Dillon

Pages 106, 107 & 109: Courtesy of McKinstry Company

Page 112: Courtesy of Costco Wholesale Corporation

Pages 115 & 117: Courtesy of Kroll Map Company

Page 120: Courtesy of Dave Rost

Page 122: Courtesy of Mike Peringer

Page 123: Courtesy of the City of Seattle

Page 124: Courtesy of Andy Yurkanin

Pages 124 & 126: Courtesy of Henry Liebman

Page 129: From "History of Seattle - Volume 1," by Clarence B. Bagley, S.J. Clarke Publishing Company, 1916

*All contemporary photos were taken by Anni Shelley

Index

Mikayla Raley

Dan Raley is a Seattle native who graduated from Roosevelt High School in 1972 and earned a journalism degree from Western Washington University in 1976. He worked at the Skagit Valley Herald in Mount Vernon, Wash., from 1974 to 1975, while attending college, and briefly at the East Washingtonian in Pomeroy, Wash., in 1976 upon graduation. Dan was the sports and outdoor editor at the Fairbanks Daily News-Miner from 1977 to 1979. He became a design editor, sportswriter, police reporter and enterprise writer at the Seattle Post-Intelligencer from 1980 to 2009. He wrote 6,000 stories for the P-I, winning 60 national, regional and Hearst awards. On January 4, 2010, he began work as a newsroom editor for the Atlanta Journal-Constitution in Georgia.